PEES & Queues

The Complete
Loo Companion

Jenny Hobbs & Tim Couzens

THE SPEARHEAD PRESS

Published by
The Spearhead Press
P O Box 75360
Gardenview, 2047
Telephone - (011) 614 1866

The Spearhead Press is a division of
Troupant Publishers (Pty) Limited
P.O. Box 3622
Pinegowrie
2123

ISBN 1 919780 58 0

First edition, first impression 1999.
First edition, second impression 2000.

Design and cover by Crazy Cat Designs
Typesetting by Crazy Cat Designs
Printed and bound by NBD
Drukkery Street, Goodwood, Western Cape

TO
THOSE FRIENDS

Who've taken the piss out of us

over the years

and,

in Tim's case,

especially

Belinda, Charles, Jill and Tony

This is our revenge.

CONTENTS

JENNY'S INTRODUCTION

About twenty years ago when I was a jobbing journalist, a publisher asked me to consider getting together a book of South African toilet trivia which he was proposing to call *The Bog Book*. Since I come from a family known for its robust humour despite my dear mother's continuous attempts to raise the tone of our gatherings, I agreed and began in a desultory way to collect news items, anecdotes, quotes, book extracts and other literature.

After a few years I presented the publisher with my initial collection plus a handful of books I owned or had bought for the purpose, including Lucinda Lambton's seminal *Temples of Convenience* and a family heirloom edition of *The Specialist*. In a subsequent move to new premises the publisher lost both the file and the books, and since he had moved on to publishing Higher Things, the project was abandoned.

The habit was established, however, and I went on collecting toilet trivia and adding to the copies of book extracts as I came across relevant passages. There was no shortage of material. To paraphrase Dorothy Sayer writing about death in *The Third Omnibus of Crime*: 'The littlest room seems to provide the minds of the Anglo-Saxon race with a greater fund of innocent amusement than any other single subject.'

Columnists regularly feature items lavatorial – and newspaper sub-editors pounce on the chance to compose droll headlines like: *FLUSHED WITH PRIDE. DRIVEN POTTY. MEET YOUR WATER-LOO. A FLASH IN THE PAN. IT'S ALL HOT AIR. SPEND A PENNY IN THE CHEAP SEATS. ROUND THE BEND. LONG-DROP TO FREEDOM. IN*

MY LADY'S CHAMBER ... and when inspiration completely failed once: OH, SH**!

Then I came across Tim Couzens' *The Seat of Learning* in the Wits Alumnus magazine *Arena*, which gave an erudite potted history of toilets, and the idea for a bog book was revived. Only this time round, it's a different publisher and a more elegant title.

Working on this book with Tim has been an extraordinary pleasure: a meeting of minds accompanied by much laughter. His love of history and literature, his thorough knowledge of sanitary matters and his pungent wit have lifted a simple collection to a higher plane – or should that read high-rise?

Whatever. It's been a privy experience, and then some.

TIM'S INTRODUCTION

When Jenny Hobbs asked me to join her on this two-seater of a book, I jumped at the chance.

On the one hand it was a privilege to collaborate with someone whose open-hearted and indefatigable advocacy of literature and literacy and whose generosity with her intellectual capital are such rare qualities in these dog eat dog days.

On the other hand it gave me the opportunity to fulfil a dream which I have long held of producing a book such as this. My involvement with the subject is not haphazard. I come from a long line of plumbers. My father was a plumber; my grandfather was a plumber. A plumbing line, if you like. I was the stupid one of the family: I became an academic (and, consequently, poor). Albert Einstein once said, 'If I had known, I would have become a plumber.' I know just how he feels.

The Holy Grail of plumbers is the perfecting of the silent cistern. According to family legend, my grandfather invented one and went to London to market it. Apparently, however, the water pressure needed for the double-storey houses did not suit his bungalow design. This is the other reason for our family's tragic decline.

My father pushed handcarts in London as an apprentice at the age of seventeen. He used to tell me proudly that he did the plumbing at the Earl of Shrewsbury's stately home of Ingester Hall in Staffordshire. I once visited it. It is now an Art School. The principal was surprised at why I was there and the kind of thing I wanted to see.

I myself once held a post at the illustrious Kings College in London. In these days of devalued and inflated curricula vitae I've often wondered whether I should include this in my academic CV. I was a porter in the men's cloakroom, hanging up coats and toilet rolls.

Now, since I have never been clever enough or lucky enough to be headhunted and to join the Brain Drain, this book seems to be the best chance I have to make a modest contribution to history by becoming a drain brain.

Many years ago I saw and fell in love with a cartoon by Don Martin in *Mad* magazine. I wish I'd kept it. It involved one of his bizarre-looking characters with overlapping feet and popping eyes in a Dr Jekyll and Mr Hyde situation. The character is in his laboratory amidst its smoking retorts, bubbling beakers and vaguely menacing carboys. He is holding a test tube containing a mysterious concoction. 'One sip of this,' he says, 'and I shall become a thing of unspeakable horror.'

He takes a sip and nothing happens. Disgusted, he throws the liquid away, into a nearby wash-hand basin. Instantly, it turns into a lavatory pan.

In a way, though, this is unfair to toilets. As human beings we are closer to them than we think, especially if we consider the opinion of that amazingly astute philosopher Christopher Morley who said, 'A human being is an ingenious assembly of portable plumbing.'

So, like the doubloon nailed to the mast in the greatest of all novels, *Moby Dick*, in which each character sees only himself, the loo is the mirror of our souls. How we interpret it, how we treat it, what we see in it, is about as good an estimation of our psyches as any psychiatrist can ever give us.

THE SOURCES

We have restricted ourselves to a few choice quotes from architectural photographer Lucinda Lambton's fascinating and erudite 1978 treatise on the toilet, *Temples of Convenience*, which made everyone look at toilets with new eyes. Expanded and updated by Pavilion in 1995, it's a must for aficionados.

Information has been gleaned from and checked with those wonderful books, *Clean and Decent* by Lawrence Wright and *Flushed with Pride* by Wallace Reyburn. Other books we have quoted from more than once include Jeremy Beadle's *Today's The Day!*, *The Toilet Book* by Bill Oddie & Laura Beaumont, *Unreliable Memoirs* by Clive James, *Privies Galore* by Mollie Harris, *A Postillion Struck by Lightning* by Dirk Bogarde, *The Moon's a Balloon* by David Niven and *Class* by Jilly Cooper. We have often found in these pioneers kindred souls and we hope they will get from our book half the pleasure, at least, that we have from theirs.

For a full list of the books from which quotes have been taken, see SELECT BIBLIOGRAPHY.

While *Pees & Queues* draws on material from around the world, it is meant to have a South African bias. Since the collecting of newspaper cuttings was mostly done in Johannesburg, quotes tend to come from *The Star* and the *Sunday Times;* they were also culled from the *Mail & Guardian*, the *Financial Mail,* Cape papers read on holiday, magazines and cuttings sent by friends. In each case we have, as far as possible, credited the publication and supplied the date of the item or the month it appeared; where there is a byline, we have credited the journalist too. Many are names that have regrettably disappeared from our newspapers; we hope you enjoy reading them again.

Columnists we have quoted more than once include Carol Lazar, Barry Ronge, John Scott, James Clarke, Gus Silber, Arnold Benjamin, Margaret de Paravicini, Robert Kirby, David Walker and Arthur Goldstuck, whom we admire greatly and thank sincerely. Jenny would also like to thank for contributions Ann and Brian Snaddon, Shirley Grindley, Barry Morton, Wendy Thorburn, Richard Holden and Adrian Davis. Tim would also like to thank for their contributions Diana Woodhouse (niece of Lawrence Wright), Diana Wall, Marita Smit (especially for her anagram), Dave Holt-Biddle, Margaret Hawker, Desmond Cole, Doug Pheasant and, above all, his friend, the late, great Nick Visser who had a *super* sense of humour.

We put *Pees & Queues* together in a matter of weeks; though gathering the material took nearly two decades. Both have been fun – a welcome break from the Serious Stuff. We hope you enjoy it as much as we have.

Jenny Hobbs and Tim Couzens, Gauteng, July 1999

The lavatory area of the Roman historical fort at
Housesteads on Hadrian's Wall
(Painting by Ronald Embleton, photograph by Diana Wall)

Roman painting by Ronald Embleton

LOO STORY
(TIM)

On the wild west coast on the main island of Orkney, north of Scotland, a storm hit the Bay of Skaill during the winter of 1850. It stripped the grass from off the high dune known as Skara Brae, uncovering a huge midden and the stone remains of a neolithic village around 5 000 years old. To this day it is an eerie privilege to stand on the site so fortuitously revealed. For the pilgrim of plumbing it is worth the long journey. A draining channel, like an altar to plumbing, provides evidence of an early water-borne sewerage system.

Further to the south snaking over the cold, bleak hills of Northumberland is the wall built by Emperor Hadrian about 120 AD. One of the forts built on the wall is now called Housesteads. At one time it must have been garrisoned by a thousand men. Of course, this meant a certain waste disposal problem. In the south-eastern corner of the fort is a finely preserved latrine. It was communal. The soldiers sat in two rows facing each other. Twin channels of water ran in front of them in which they dipped the sponges which they used in the absence of Kleenex. The water in these channels was then diverted below their seats to flush away to a point a hundred yards to the south (on the English side!)

Letter from Professor Desmond Cole to Tim:

Your article reminded me of the multi-seater (12-20 seats) waterborne public loo which I saw in 1942, in the Roman ruins near Homs, east of Tripoli. I wonder if they are still there – they were in excellent condition then, but the last 50 years have seen devastation of everything worthwhile in the world at an ever escalating pace. The seats were all beautifully carved in stone, with a water channel below, and arranged in a semicircle. It must have been a great place to sit and relax and chat in Latin about the events of the day! Unfortunately, I did not get any pictures - we were far too busy running after Rommel, who, not many months before, had been running after us!

When the Normans came they built castles all over England and Wales. This was in 1066 and All That had to be disposed of. The mediaeval name for the loo was the garderobe (from the French 'garder' meaning to keep and 'robe' meaning dress). It was usually a simple stone seat or platform, perched high up in the battlements overhanging the moat. They were often windy in more ways than one and somewhat hazardous when the castle was under attack, especially when the enemy was using arrows. Often, since many castles were strategically placed along the coast, the garderobes hovered over the sea giving the opportunity for its inhabitants to revenge themselves on any low-flying gulls. The majestic ruin of Tantallon Castle on the Scottish east coast presents a fine example.

Over the centuries – even over millennia – sanitation went backwards rather than forwards. The first historian of the process, Lawrence Wright, was scathing about the Dark Ages, suggesting the alternative title of Dirt Ages. Castles which had previously been defensive had now, he suggests, become offensive. Let him, like Dante's Virgil, take us by the hand into the underworld of sanitation.

He points out that while the Romans had, in the fourth century AD, 11 public baths (one six times the floor area of St Paul's Cathedral), 1 352 public fountains and 144 public water-flushed latrines, and could deliver 300 gallons of water per head per day (compared with 51 gallons per head in England in the 1960s), eight hundred years later King John was comparatively diligent in taking a bath every three weeks. Four hundred years on little progress had been made: Elizabeth I took a bath, once a month, 'whether she need it or no'.

When no water was available, movable barrels or cesspits or what-have-you had to do. With houses on London Bridge there was a hazardous undertaking known as 'shooting the bridge', and the saying developed that the bridge was 'for wise men to go over and for fools to go under'. The removers of nightsoil from pits were known as gongfermors; at Queenborough Castle in 1375 the gentlemen entrusted to this task rejoiced in the names of William Mokkyng and Nicholas Richeandgood. Stairs were often spiral to prevent soiling in the corners.

GONGFERMORS:
gong from the Saxon 'gong' meaning 'to go off', and 'fey' from the Saxon word 'to cleanse'.

EVO - LOO - TION

As stately houses came to replace the more spartan castles, so elegance replaced austerity and necessity. Loos became part of the furniture – literally. By the sixteenth century the 'closed stool' became the main alternative to the garderobe: 'cosier for the user,' comments Wright wryly, 'but hard on the servants.' Sometimes padded or lined with the Elizabethan equivalent of fun fur, these pieces of furniture were germ-traps of exquisite proportions. Commodes were disguised as chairs and desks and cabinets. The late sixteenth century tower-house of Lauriston in Edinburgh contains several excellent specimens.

We are also given a tantalising glimpse of a plumbing pioneer, surely worth a full biography. In 1596 Sir John Harington wrote his *Metamorphosis of Ajax: A Cloacinean Satire* in which he set out his valve water closet invention nearly 300 years before its Victorian successor. A prophet before his time, but no profit in his time.

Being a Renaissance man (of the European variety) he also put his hand to poetry, suitably moral in its functions:

A godly father, sitting on a draught
    To do as need and nature hath us taught,
Mumbled (as was his manner) certain prayers,
    And unto him the devil straight repairs,
And boldly to revile him he begins,
    Alleging that such prayers were deadly sins
And that he shewed he was devoid of grace
    To speak to God from so unmeet a place.

The reverent man, though at first dismayed,
    Yet strong in faith, to Satan thus he said:
Thou damnéd spirit, wicked, false and lying,
    Despairing thine own good, and ours envying,
Each take his due, and me thou canst not hurt,
    To God my prayer I meant, to thee the dirt.
Pure prayer ascends to Him that high doth sit,
    Down falls the filth, for fiends of hell more fit.

There was no marked improvement in the seventeenth century since Milton seems to be speaking straight from the heart and long experience when he wrote in Book I of *Paradise Lost*:

As one who long in populous city pent,
Where houses thick and sewers annoy the air,
Forth issuing on a summer's morn to breath
Among the pleasant villages and farms
Adjoin'd, from each thing met conceives delight.

Nor was there in the eighteenth century. It was probably from early in that century (when the Fleet river ran down the centre of Fleet Street in London and acted as an open sewer) that the word 'loo' came into existence. G M Trevelyan in his eighteenth century volume of *English Social History* gives a graphic description of Edinburgh at the time:

> On six evenings of the week the taverns were filled with men of all classes at their ale and claret, till the ten o'clock drum, beaten at the order of the magistrates, warned every man that he must be off home. Then were the High Street and Canongate filled with parties of every description, hurrying unsteadily along, High Court judges striving to walk straight as became their dignity, rough Highland porters swearing in Gaelic as they forced a passage for their sedan-chairs, while far overhead the windows opened, five, six or ten storeys in the air, and the close stools of Edinburgh discharged the collected filth of the last twenty-four hours into the street. It was good manners for those above to cry 'Gardy-loo' (Gardez l'eau) before throwing. The returning roysterer cried back, 'Haud yer han' and ran with humped shoulders, lucky if his fast and expensive full-bottomed wig was not put out of action by a cataract of filth. The ordure thus sent down lay in the broad High Street and in the deep, well-like closes and wynds around it making the night air horrible, until early in the morning it was perfunctorily cleaned away by the City Guard. Only on a Sabbath morn it might not be touched, but lay there all day long, filling Scotland's capital with the savour of a mistaken piety.

The novelist Thomas Smollett in *Humphrey Clinker* gives us a similar but contemporary eighteenth century description in one of his characters' letters:

> And now, dear Mary, we have got to Haddinborrough, among the Scots, who are civil enuff for our money, thof I don't speak their lingo. But they should not go for to impose upon foreigners; for the bills in their houses say, they have different easements to let; and behold there is nurro geaks in the whole kingdom, nor any thing for poor sarvants, but a barrel with a pair of tongs thrown a-cross; and all the chairs in the family are emptied into this here barrel once a-day; and at ten o'clock at night the whole cargo is flung out of a back windore that looks into some street or lane, and the maid calls gardy loo to the passengers, which signified Lord have mercy upon you! and this is done every night in every house in Haddinborough...

There are other explanations of the origins of the word. One possibility is the anglicised form of the French 'lieu' – meaning 'the place'. Another possibility favoured in the present day is that it derives from 'Waterloo'. An attractive one, however, is to be found in the *Penguin Dictionary of the Decorative Arts*:

> The bordalou, much used in the eighteenth century by ladies travelling or in other privy difficulties on drawn-out social occasions. Portable in a muff, its artistic quality and its shape have sometimes led to its being mistaken nowadays for a sauce-boat. The name is said to derive from Louis Bourdaloue, the fashionable and prolix Jesuit preacher of Louis XIV's reign. The first known example, made in

Delft, dates from 1710 – and the article became very much 'the thing'.

Bordaloue's sermons were reputedly so long-winded that many ladies found such a contrivance necessary. Yet other ideas of where the word comes from are 'leeward' since that is, on a small boat, the side one would use, or from 'ablution'.

ANOTHER CASE OF MISTAKEN IDENTITY

It's not only financial experts that get it wrong sometimes. The catalogue for Stephan Welz's decorative arts auction next week includes an item described as 'A pair of Georgian silver strainers'.

Somewhat shamefacedly, the firm admitted that its London associate, Sothebys, has pointed out that they are, in fact, 'a pair of nipple shields for use by professional wet nurses'!

– *Financial Mail,* 18 September 1992

Whatever the name it should be noted, however, that a certain dignity was attached to the Royal Stool, especially on the continent, and it was the scene of many dramatic events. It was often treated literally as a throne before which audiences took place. Lord Portland, the English Ambassador to the Court of Louis XIV, was summoned to this particular throne from which the king announced his marriage to Mme de Maintenon! A King of Naples had a heart attack and died while sitting on his 'throne', as did George II of England.

PORT – À – LOO

> Despite foreign ridicule, France has pioneered many developments in sanitation. These include the superloo – the high-tech public lavatory that cleans itself after each use – and the bidet, invented in 1672 by the Frenchman Auguste Bidet as a therapeutic device to treat his own syphilis.
>
> – Bush Telegraph, *Daily Telegraph*, 26 July 1997

The bidet (coming from a French word meaning a small horse which is easily straddled) first appears in England about 1710 but, as Lawrence Wright notes, was still so unfamiliar by the late 1730s that one dealer mistook its function and advertised it as 'a porcelain violin-case with four legs'. At that time it was not a fixture but a movable piece of furniture with a bowl that was filled with warm water from jugs and later emptied by the servants.

The night commode or jerry had its ancient ancestors but begins to appear in modern form about the fourteenth century. One of its most distinguished appearances (or rather, non-appearances) was in the Speaker's chair in the House of Commons where a silver pot was concealed so that the Speaker could be present for the entire session and remain po-faced throughout.

By the late nineteenth century some jerries came with concealed musical boxes which played 'appropriate chamber music'. Some, apparently, even played trumpet music.

The commode gets an anonymous walk-on part in Canto One of Byron's poem *Don Juan*. While hero Don Juan, having been seduced by the fair Donna Julia, lies asleep in her arms, her husband Don Alfonso rushes in with curses on his lips and hell in his heart. Nimble-witted Julia flings the bedclothes and Juan into one indistinguishable heap:

He search'd, they search'd and rummaged
  everywhere,
Closet and clothes-press, chest and window-seat,
And found much linen, lace, and several pair
Of stockings, slippers, brushes, combs, complete,
With other articles of ladies fair,
To keep them beautiful, or leave them neat:
Arras they prick'd and curtains with their swords,
And wounded several shutters, and some boards.

Under the bed they search'd, and there they found –
No matter what – it was not that they sought;
They open'd windows, gazing if the ground
Had signs or footmarks, but the earth said nought;
And then they stared each other's faces round:
'Tis odd, not one of all these seekers thought,
And seems to me almost a sort of blunder,
Of looking in the bed as well as under.

LITERARY BLOOMERS

If we do not know what Scotsmen wore under their kilts, we do know what women wore under their dresses until fairly recent times. Nothing. Under-drawers were in their infancy in 1850 when a pioneering American social reformer called Amelia Bloomer introduced long loose trousers gathered at the ankle and worn under a shorter skirt, which soon took her name. No doubt because of their voluminous character and embarrassment potential, the name came, by metaphoric extension or some other route, to mean an embarrassing faux pas.

If the feminine origin is appropriate, then it is fair to point to one of the more embarrassing bloomers in literature – from none other than Jane Austen *and* in *Pride and Prejudice*:

> On entering the room, she found the whole party at loo, and was immediately invited to join them...
>
> **(Quoted from Bodley Head's *A New Garden of Bloomers*)**

For a writer so sure of her touch, so delicate in sensibility, this is a lapse of monumental proportions.

Even the Poet Laureate himself, Alfred, Lord Tennyson, sometimes let his knickers show, as in his well-known poem *Locksley Hall*:

> In the spring a young man's fancy lightly turns to thoughts of love.
> Then her cheek was pale and thinner than should be for one so young,
> And her eyes on all my motions with a mute observance hung.

Humorist Frank Muir has suggested the poem might have been inspired by a two-seater loo. No wonder her cheek was pale.

Imagine, too, the sensation that would be caused if any Royal Shakespeare Company director took literally the words of the sentry, Francisco, in *Hamlet* when he says at the beginning of the play, 'For this relief, much thanks.' Especially if the ramparts of Elsinore Castle overlooked the first row of the stalls.

T S Eliot: an anagram of toilets

SANITATION SAGA

Lawrence Wright (who, incidentally, was also a brilliant architect responsible for some of the work in Guildford Cathedral) reminds us that there is a deadly serious side to the whole topic of sanitation. He points out that although the population of London increased by half between 1750 and 1800, the death rate actually fell.

But it was still extremely high in nineteenth century England. Of 1 000 children under five, 240 died in the country and 480 in the city – nearly half! The Fleet Ditch was as filthy in 1840 as it was in 1340; a year later in 1841 it was covered at last. Although Richard II had introduced a statute which forbade dung-dumping, the first public health act dealing with closets in England was only introduced in 1848; it made illegal the building of any house without a sufficient WC or privy or ashpit (with a fine of £20 for non-compliance).

By 1830 cholera had spread from India and reached western Russia. At first it was thought 'incapable of attacking a decent Englishman, until it struck London with sensational effect in 1832, and again at intervals until 1866.' (In 1849, 14 000 died of it; in 1854, over 10 000; in 1866, 5 000). Initially people didn't realise that cholera was waterborne and being spread by wells contaminated by cesspits; in 1850 there were still 80 000 waterless houses in London. It was only when a doctor noticed that cholera occurred within a radius of certain wells that the fact began to sink in and the wells were closed over.

To give an indication of what early Victorian conditions meant to the man in the street, we need only refer to a letter from William Knott in 1840 which was written as part of the ongoing agitation following the 1831 cholera epidemic in Sunderland:

> I beg respectfully to make known to you a serious existing abuse viz: – the fact that the street lamps are extinguished generally two or three hours before daylight at this time of the year which is a source of considerable danger... There are some awkwardly-situated public privies adjoining the river; four men have been drowned within a short space of time when going to these early in the morning, the lamps being out at the time; and I know, from personal observations, that individual collisions, and consequent brawls, are of frequent occurrence.

In the 1870s the death rate began to fall decisively, and who do we have to thank? Largely, the Chief Engineer of the London Board of Works, Joseph Bazalgette, who not only constructed both the Albert and Victoria Embankments but also the vast drainage and sewerage system that was completed by 1865. Hail to thee, Joseph Bazalgette! Hero of our time.

THE GOLDEN AGE

We now come to the high-water mark of loos – the late Victorian Age. At last we emerge from the circles of hell and a world of purgatory to glimpse a new heaven. And here, together with Lawrence Wright, we are joined by a new guide in the person of Wallace Reyburn, author of the eminently readable *Flushed with Pride : The Story of Thomas Crapper*.

When Queen Victoria came to the throne (the real throne, we hasten to add) in 1837, there was no bathroom in Buckingham Palace. This was soon remedied. George Jennings insisted, despite opposition, that the Crystal Palace be fitted with loos for the Great Exhibition of 1851 and no fewer than 827 280 people paid for their use. (To Jennings, therefore, we owe the expression 'spending a penny', and largely to Jennings do we owe that useful place, the public convenience). The Crystal Palace loos were a sensation that effectively spread the word of modern sanitation and Prince Albert, ever appreciative of scientific advances, had some installed at once.

ALAS

Joseph Bazalgette's sewerage system was not finished in time to save Prince Albert, Queen Victoria's husband, who died of typhoid in 1861.

The Golden Age of loos begins in 1870, the *annus mirabilis* of loos. (Note to printer: beware of dropping one n by mistake).

For nearly a hundred years Joseph Bramah's valve closet had performed yeoman service. But in 1870 T W Twyford produced his Washout Closet; Hellyer the 'Optimus' Improved Valve Closet; and J R Mann the 'Epic' Syphonic Closet. Jennings's 'Pedestal Vase' was able to flush regularly at one sitting – no flush in the pan, this – no fewer than 10 apples, 1 flat sponge, plumber's 'smudge' coated over the pan and 4 pieces of paper. Mr Shanks (remember the graffiti on many urinals next to his trade name: 'No Shanks, I don't shink I oughter?') went even further at a demonstration of one new model by snatching a cap off an apprentice's head, throwing it in and pulling the chain, happily crying, 'It works!' as the cap disappeared.

In 1885 the hitherto shameful loo finally came out of the closet. Porcelain maker Twyford brought out his 'Unitas' model – no longer encased, no longer disguised as a chair, a cupboard, or surrounded by woodwork. The thing itself: pure, pristine. The advantage? It could be easily cleaned and did not trap dirt in unwanted corners. It also provided, according to Wallace Reyburn, a way for British subjects to show their loyalty:

> The Angel Hotel in Doncaster was among the first proud possessors of a 'Unitas' and the management were even more proud when Queen Victoria on a visit to the town made use of it. Wishing to capitalise on this, they were placed in rather a quandary. Numerous inns around the country displayed notices to the effect that 'Queen Elizabeth Slept Here' but they could not very well make capital out of Queen Victoria's brief visit by erecting a sign on something of the same lines. However, it did not become necessary. Word of mouth, as ever, proving the best form of advertising, the news soon got around and each day saw the ladies of Doncaster making their way to the Angel and queuing up to use the same toilet that had been graced by their beloved Queen.

And then we have a last, great Hero: the man who developed the modern WC cistern. Wallace Reyburn explains:

> In the old days the water for a flushing toilet was provided from a cistern in which there was a valve at the outlet to the flush pipe. When you pulled the chain it simply lifted up that valve and released the water. In other words, you just pulled the plug out. Some people would tie the chain down so

that the valve was perpetually open and the water flowed ceaselessly.

Obviously, the waste of water was prodigious as no valve ever worked properly. So the modern cistern was developed with its 'Pull and Let Go' action. The name of the inventor was Thomas Crapper.

After apprenticing himself to a London plumber in 1847 at the age of eleven, he had established his own business by 1861: Thomas Crapper & Co, Marlborough Works, Chelsea. He lived in Chelsea with other artists like Turner, Rossetti and Whistler and did much of the plumbing at Sandringham House (built by Prince Albert for Edward, Prince of Wales) and at Westminster Abbey. Crapper also devised ways to cut down on the curse of the loos – noise.

You may not have thought about it much, but there are at least four distinct noises connected with the domestic thunderbox which Reyburn identifies:

1. The sound of the flush itself – the downrush of water to the pan.

2. The gurgle which occurs at the end of the flush.

3. The hissing sound of the water coming in to refill the cistern.

4. The noise of water coming under high pressure to the cistern through the pipes.

Every time you hardly hear the loo, think of the silencers fitted (known collectively as the Marlboro Silent Water Waste Preventer) and offer up a hymn of thanks to Thomas Crapper. And if you are inclined to dismiss this achievement, please remember the story from *Time* magazine retold by Crapper's biographer:

At the coronation of our present Queen the organisers of the occasion were concerned, among other things, about the matter of the special needs of the great number of Peers who would be assembled at Westminster Abbey, many of whom were well on in years and not able, with the best will in the world, to stay settled in one place for long periods, as the lengthy ceremony demanded. It was known that the very aptly named 'peer's bladder' would come to their aid, but there was more to it than that. So an additional 'range' of toilets, as they call it in the trade, had to be installed to cope with the expected increased demand.

Then somebody got the frightening thought that at the vital moment of the ceremony, when the whole Abbey would be in hushed silence as the crown was being placed on the Queen's head, there might be one of those terrible coincidences whereby all the toilets happened to be occupied and all their occupants pulled the chain at the same time.

Would the strains of that symphonic flush penetrate into the body of the Abbey and create one of the major embarrassments in the history of British Royalty? There was nothing for it but to have a test.

A detachment of Guards from nearby Wellington Barracks was pressed into service, and as technicians borrowed from the BBC, each armed with a decibel meter, were stationed at various key points in the main part of the Abbey, the troops were deployed along the long line of toilets. It is not known what form of drill was evolved for this unique exercise. It was probably something like: 'At the command, "Chains – PULL" … wait for it!' Anyway, as the order rang out all the toilets were flushed simultaneously and the good news from inside the Abbey was that nothing could be heard of the noises off. The heading *Time* magazine put on their story about it was ROYAL FLUSH.

So Crapper and Twyford have given us the loo as we know it today – the pan and the cistern, separate but equal.

DID 'CRAP' DERIVE FROM CRAPPER?

The *Oxford English Dictionary* says that crap means the husk of grain or chaff, a name of some plants – buckwheat and rye grass – the residue formed from boiling fat, the dregs of beer or ale, money and so on. There is no mention of rubbish or shit. The second edition admits, as the seventh meaning, excrement, defecation (coarse slang), with a first use in 1898, and the verb 'to crap' meaning to defecate, in use since 1846.

In the US, 'crapper' means lavatory; one theory is that the word was brought back by American troops serving in Britain during the First World War who were impressed by Thomas Crapper's products. But if the word 'crap' was used to mean defecate as far back as 1846, Thomas Crapper cannot have been responsible, since he was only ten years old at the time.

– From *Thunder, Flush and Thomas Crapper* by Adam Hart-Davis

---

DOIN' WHAT COMES
NATURALLY

> Folks are dumb
> Where I come from
> They ain't had any learnin'
> Still, they're happy as can be
> Doin' what comes naturally.
>
> — *Irving Berlin*

Bodily functions being a taboo subject in polite society until quite recently, the paradox of the sublime Mozart's foul language and obsession with anal matters has always puzzled the genteel music world. According to Liz Hunt, writing in the English *Independent* in December 1992:

> Many of his letters and some of his lyrics reveal a startling vulgarity, which had to be censored after his death by his wife, Constanze... In one letter to his father, Mozart describes how he entertained the director of the world-famous Mannheim orchestra by reciting obscene rhymes on such subjects as 'muck, shitting and arse-licking'.

Researchers in the Department of Medicine at the Cedars-Sinai Medical Centre in Los Angeles, who analysed his letters and contemporary descriptions of his behaviour, now believe that he suffered from Tourette's syndrome, which causes jerking and nervous tics and sudden outbursts of obscenities which the sufferers of the syndrome are unable to control. In some people (and this is the really interesting bit) the condition is linked to extraordinary memory and a profound artistic or creative drive.

Society is no longer polite. Bodily functions are the mainstay of stand-up comics, discussed over café tables and analysed in microscopic detail in magazine articles, all in the cause of good health. We are enjoined to eat less fat and more fibre for our bowels, to drink more water for our kidneys and bladders, to sweat freely when we exercise.

'KYBO!' is a common injunction to the infirm or elderly, and it was Oliver Cromwell who seems to have said it first: 'Work hard, trust in God and keep your bowels open.'

John Harvey Kellogg, who invented cornflakes, was a worthy successor to Cromwell. He was so obsessed with bodily functions, reported the *Sunday Times* on 27 November 1994, that it became his mission to solve the world's digestive problems. He believed 'clean bowels made for clean thoughts' and 'universal constipation' was the 'most destructive blockade that has ever opposed human progress'. He even 'personally inquired of the directors of the London and Bronx Zoos how often their primates moved their bowels.'

His secret weapon in the crusade for bodily purity was the enema, and the rich and famous flocked to his sanitarium in Battle Creek, Michigan, to have their bowels irrigated. Johnny Weissmuller, Roald Amundsen, Thomas Edison, Amelia Earhart and Henry Ford all made the health pilgrimage to Battle Creek in search of purified plumbing. Since Kellogg also believed that 'sex is the sewer drain of a healthy body', his patients can't have had much fun there – though we can, watching the hilarious movie *The Road to Wellville* which documents his eccentric life.

QUESTION: What literary classic begins with one of the main characters worried about his bowel movements? See end of chapter for answer.

THE PASSING SHOW

Dr Martyn Gorman, a chemist at Aberdeen University, told the Edinburgh International Science Festival in April 1996 that dung, sweat and urine not only arouse the ardour of animals from hyenas to deer, but can also inflame the passions of people. Many of the scents animals use to identify members of their own species are now used in perfumes by men and women who would be horrified at their origin.

Roman women imported hyena faeces from Africa to powder their faces. In the Middle Ages a scent secreted by a gland in the anus of a civet cat was used as an aphrodisiac in the finest perfumes and a contemporary advertisement claimed: 'Civet will cause (so) much desire for a wife that she will almost continually wish to make love to her husband.'

Musk comes from a gland directly above the Himalayan musk deer's penis and ambergris comes from the intestines of sperm whales...

(From a Reuter report, April 1996)

Archaeologists have a particular interest in excreta:

ANCIENT LOO YIELDS RICH HARVEST

A seventeenth century privy in Oxford is providing archaeologists with a revealing insight into the diet of a wealthy household 300 years ago.

The loo was discovered when an old fireplace was demolished two years ago, revealing an underground chamber (with) ... nearly four tons of damp fibrous brown material, decayed faeces. It had been used as a privy by Robert Say, Provost of Oriel from 1653 and his wife Anne Zouch.

The provost's diet was exceptionally rich. Remains of fruit seeds show that he ate cherries, wild strawberries, raspberries, plums, gooseberries and mulberries. He also had grapes and figs, which would have been imported from Greece. Traces of mustard and fennel seeds suggest that these were used to flavour the provost's food. There were also black peppers, probably cooked whole in stews, which would have been shipped from Java.

(From *The Observer*, January 1984)

But such investigations are not confined to archaeologists:

> WASHINGTON, December 1987 – The decision by Mr Gorbachev to sleep at the Soviet Embassy here and not in accommodation provided by the US Government has stymied plans by the CIA to collect a bit of intelligence on the state of his health.
>
> According to columnist Jack Anderson, the CIA had been plotting how to collect a stool sample from the Soviet leader.
>
> In a similar indelicate manoeuvre, Britain's MI6 tried unsuccessfully to get a stool sample when the Gorbachevs visited London two years ago.
>
> Anderson says the CIA reached the heights of espionage success when they filched some faeces from Nikita Kruschev during his 1959 visit to the US and concluded he was in excellent health for a man of his age and portliness.
>
> **(With acknowledgement to Arnold Benjamin's *So it goes...* column in *The Star*, 9 December 1987)**

For the ecologically-conscious, excreta are seen as a valuable resource. Andy Fourie, an associate professor in the environmental engineering department at Wits, wrote in the *Weekend Star* in November 1994:

We have another human waste product that is unexploited: sewage. It's not exactly a dinner party conversation topic, but what do we do with this human waste once it has been collected and treated?

We should be considering co-composting, a process widely used in Malaysia, China and Thailand. It involves blending sewage sludge with domestic garbage and piling it up in large rows, through which air is forced.

Once the little resident supercharged bacteria get going on this delectable cocktail, their frenetic activities generate lots of heat, with temperatures rising to as much as 65° C.

This kills the bugs such as salmonella and within about three weeks our pile of unmentionable becomes a sweet-smelling and nutrient-rich compost.

The need to dispose of large quantities of noxious material no longer exists. Instead, a resource is created which could be sold or even given away... In impoverished rural areas it could be the saviour of poorly fertilised crops, remembering all the while we are dealing with a benign, nutrient-rich resource.

The problem is, quite simply, attitude. People don't find it an appealing thought... Just imagine biting into a juicy tomato grown in...

The Japanese have a more salubrious use for the by-products of excreta. Alan Robinson reported in the *Saturday Star*, 21 November 1992:

FROM SEWAGE, A GIRL'S BEST FRIEND

Jewellery has saved many a husband's turkey, preserved many a young man's engagement and brought many a sparkle to a fledgling romance.

But in these days of unemployment and recession, rings and things are beyond many a depleted pocket.

Now the Japanese have come up with cheap jewellery that is indistinguishable from the bank-breaking real thing. And they've sent some examples of 'metro-marble' trinkets to Britain's Southern Water Authority. How odd, but read on.

Southern Water is mightily impressed with its light and dark-grey stones set in silver pendants. They could swear they were made of onyx and pearl. 'You would have to say there is no way you would know what it was originally,' says a spokesman.

Until you look at the name of the sender, that is. It's the Sewage Bureau of Tokyo, the body which handles human waste in the world's busiest city.

The 'metro-marble' is made from slag as a by-product of sewage sludge incineration. Most of it is turned into paving slabs and building bricks, although some has been used to produce a nice line in pottery. But the best is saved for those sparklers.

Southern Water is interested because in 1998 it will become illegal in Britain to dump sewage into the sea and they will have to burn the stuff. Sniffing a lucrative domestic market, Southern Water contacted Ratners jewellery chain to discuss a possible joint venture. They were not amused.

And then there's the question of regularity:

> There are three things you need in life: respect for all kinds of life, a nice bowel movement on a regular basis and a blue blazer.
>
> – Robin Williams in *The Fisher King*

Paul Getty, to his children:
After an expensive meal, delay going to the toilet as long as you can so as to get the maximum benefit.

PISST ...

Urine has been given a number of names in English down the years – strang, chamberlye, pizzle, old swill, scour and slop – which reflect its various uses.

'Urine's been *important*,' Corinne Julius explained in a 1994 UK radio programme, *Now Wash Your Hands.* 'For centuries it was the only source of ammonia for bleach and household cleaning. And British industry could not have developed without the contents of the slop bucket.' Reporting on the programme, Libby Purves of *The Times* wrote:

> In the seventeenth century ships used to carry 4 000 gallons at a time from London to Whitby for the alum industry, and down the centuries it has softened wool, hardened steel, tanned leather, dyed cloth as well as beautified skin. The purple band on the Roman soldier's toga owed its brilliance to lichen marinated in stale wee; courtesans in sixteenth century Venice soaked their hair in it, draped it over the brim of a crownless hat and sat in the sun to develop bright Titian-red locks. The artists who painted them mixed it with inks and pigments and plaster...
>
> There are people living who well remember the value of urine. Not only was it used to de-grease wool in commercial mills well into this century,

but engineers routinely used it for rust-jointing slack machine wheels. 'I remember an old man fixing this driving-wheel which kept working loose,' said one mill-hand. 'He said, clear the area of all the women – I'm going to pumice it down and pee on it. And he did. And he said, that won't come loose now, the acid binds the two pieces of metal together. It worked.'

Midwives remember routinely wiping babies' faces with wet nappies for the sake of their skin. In the First World War it was used in makeshift gas masks and to disinfect wounds. Clay Jones remembers having a thimbleful poured into his ear to cure earache as a little boy (it worked: 'the problem was getting it into the thimble'). A hair salon in Australia developed a setting lotion based on it, and well they might: old barbers used 'lye', which was nothing else... Old wives believed that if you soaked a man's socks in your urine, he would fall in love with you.

And of course, many people – including former Indian Prime Minister Morarji Desai – ascribe their longevity to drinking the stuff.

In Lancashire there were many ancient remedies for sicknesses. For warts and other excrescences on the neck, the touch of a dead man's hand was a sure-fire cure. For whooping cough, a child should be passed nine times around the neck of a she-ass. And until late into the nineteenth century, children in that county were still cured of bed-wetting by being fed fried mice.

The exhibition of Queen Victoria's clothes at the London Museum in 1997 was fascinating for many reasons. She was a tiny, slender young woman who grew squatter with age until she looked like a dumpy frog, and her dresses ranged from a young girl's frivolous frocks to the black widow's weeds she wore after her beloved Albert died.

Her intimate underwear was always dainty: fine lawn camisoles and petticoats trimmed with tucking and lace – and voluminous drawers without crotches, held up by drawstrings at the waist. We wonder if they were designed that way because of a need for speed in alleviating the problem described by Muriel Spark in *Memento Mori*?

> The real rise of democracy in the British Isles occurred in Scotland by means of Queen Victoria's bladder... When she went to stay at Balmoral in her latter years a number of privies were caused to be built at the backs of little cottages which had not previously possessed privies. This was to enable the Queen to go on her morning drive round the countryside in comfort, and to descend from her carriage from time to time, ostensibly to visit the humble cottagers in their dwellings. Eventually, word went round that Queen Victoria was exceedingly democratic. Of course it was all due to her little weakness. But everyone copied the Queen and the idea spread, and now you see we have a great democracy.

The pee problem faced by men as they grow older is summed up in two words: enlarged prostates. According to John Soderlund writing in a business publication in 1992, it is the prime time-waster among older men in the office, costing international business billions every year:

Ronald Reagan, Helmut Kohl and Bob Hawke suffered from it.

Harold Macmillan had it so bad he thought it was cancer and resigned as Britain's Prime Minister – only to live another 25 years with faulty waterworks. Chances are you too suffer from an enlarged prostate gland if you are male and over 50 years of age, and if you do, you will know what it is like to have to sneak off to the Gentlemen every 45 minutes. Statistics say 50% of men over 50, 60% over 60 and 70% over 70 have to step out of the office more often than they like...

It is all caused by a walnut-sized gland just below the bladder and surrounding the urethra, or urinary tube. For reasons still unclear to the medical profession, the gland begins to enlarge around the age of 40 until it exerts pressure on the urethra, restricting the flow of urine. Men find themselves in embarrassing situations in the boardroom, on the road to the job or just meeting other aging executives in the toilet more often than behind their desks.

There is hope for sufferers, however: either a brief procedure which opens up the urethra or prostate surgery usually relieves the problem. (And savvy men over 40 also have regular PSA blood tests which can pick up prostate cancer in its earliest stages).

The real problem, doctors say, is that men find this intimate predicament so difficult to talk about that they'll wait until it's severe before doing anything about it. Sometimes with dire consequences.

One of the most touching descriptions of aging men's pee problems comes from *Love in the Time of Cholera* by Gabriel Garcia Marquez:

He was the first man that Fermina Daza heard urinate. She heard him on their wedding night ... and the sound of his stallion's stream seemed so potent, so replete with authority, that it increased her terror of the devastation to come. That memory often returned to her as the years weakened the stream, for she never could resign herself to his wetting the rim of the toilet bowl each time he used it.

Dr Urbino tried to convince her ... that the mishap was not repeated every day through carelessness on his part, as she insisted, but because of organic reasons: as a young man his stream was so defined and so direct that when he was at school he won contests for marksmanship in filling bottles, but with the ravages of age it was not only decreasing, it was also becoming oblique and scattered, and had at last turned into a fantastic fountain, impossible to control despite his many efforts to direct it. He would say: 'The toilet must have been invented by someone who knew nothing about men.' He contributed to domestic peace with a quotidian act that was more humiliating than humble: he wiped the rim of the bowl with toilet paper each time he used it.

The actor David Niven had a different kind of wee problem when he attended his first regimental dinner, described in his autobiography *The Moon's a Balloon*:

Round after round of drinks in the anteroom and finally just as I was headed for a most necessary trip to the lavatory, Mr Gifford announced dinner. Like a lamb to the slaughter, I was led with bursting bladder to my chair next to my Commanding Officer. As he had still not spoken to me directly during my service, I was in no position to ask him if I might be excused, an unthinkable request as officers and gentlemen never left the table under any circumstances until the end of the meal when the King's health had been drunk. Sweat broke out all over me as I contemplated the hours of agony ahead...

I sat in miserable silence with crossed legs, perspiration trickling down inside my stiff shirt front, my stand-up wing collar wilting with pain. Cold soup (more strain on the bladder) was followed by other courses, each washed down by a different wine. I drank everything that was placed in front of me in the vague hope that something might act as an anaesthetic and reduce the torture.

By the time we arrived at the cheese, I was desperate, past caring. As far as I was concerned my career could end in a pool right there under the polished mahogany and the regimental silver, but succour was at hand. Mr Gifford bent over and whispered in my ear, 'With Mr Trubshawe's compliments, sir, I have just placed an empty magnum underneath your chair.' Relief, when I heard his words, did not flow over me – it spurted out of me. In an apparently endless stream, but thanks to a firm grip on the bottle with my knees, I was able to aim with one hand and leave the other available to crumble, nonchalantly, a water biscuit. This proved just as well because suddenly the Colonel zeroed in on me and spoke to me for the first time. I was so unnerved by this sudden reversal of form that I nearly released my grip on the warm and by now heavy receptacle below the table.

His words were few and his point was made with admirable clarity. 'I have,' he said, 'fucked women of every nationality and most animals, but the one thing I cannot abide is a girl with a Glasgow accent. Pass the port.' He never spoke to me again.

Another young man made excellent use of his capacity. An Edinburgh Festival in the late 1980s welcomed what was described as its 'first genuine piss artist': John Cousins (no relation), a New Zealand music lecturer from Canterbury University who took *Membrane*, his seven-hour performance show, to the Festival fringe. The news item read:

In the course of the show Mr Cousins drinks 18 to 20 mouthfuls of water at a time and ... urinates on a series of rubber membranes to create drum-like sounds and noises.

He has said the inspiration for *Membrane* comes from the simplest of sources – the sound of dripping water heard in a New Zealand canyon. 'I am the biological material in the work,' he explained.

From Abbot Feckenham's *Book of sovereigne medicines against the most common and knowne diseases, chiefly for the poor, who have not at all times the learned phisitions at hande, 1515-84:*

A MEDECYNE TO PURGE THE BLADDER OF HIM THAT CANNOT PISSE:

Take fennell the leaves and the rootes, alledanders, parceley the leaves and the rootes, hartstonnge, mayden heare, and seethe them in white wyne, and give it to the patient to drinke. It shall purge the bladder in short tyme.

('seethe' – the old word for extracting the essence of a food by boiling)

... AND WIND

Undoubtedly the quickest way to raise a laugh in the English-speaking world is to let off a fart. Whoopee cushions have the same effect but do not produce quite the same expressions of rude glee among onlookers.

The Cockneys called them 'raspberry tarts', as explained in the *Dictionary of Rhyming Slang* by Julian Franklyn:

> Polite people, who would not care to use so vulgar a medium of expression as rhyming slang, and who would never even think so robust a word as fart, will use the word raspberry to describe a mild admonition or gentle expression of disapproval.

The pseudonymous 'Phil A Page' in the *Sunday Star* of 18 October 1992 pointed out that the SABC had 'Unveiled its secret weapon in the war against pirate viewers. "From all those who have paid their television licences," ran the ad this week, "to all those who haven't..." Cut to one red raspberry, resplendent on a spotlit pedestal.'

TOMBSTONE IN LEYLAND CHURCHYARD IN LANCASHIRE:

Let the wind go free
Where'er you be
For 'twas the wind
That killed me.

– From Arnold Silcock's *Verse and Worse*

As a weapon, the fart has a definite advantage. Simon Hoggart of *The Observer,* in a July 1990 article about giving up smoking, suggested:

> I think that the answer (to people who insist on smoking) may lie in the grand old tradition of the fart. We all fart, it's a natural, even pleasurable function, and nothing to be ashamed of. It has much

in common with smoking, being offensive not to the practitioner but only to the people around him.

So next time someone lights up near your lunch, move round and let out a real rip-snorter, a high pressure blast of methane which could take out a hectare hole in the ozone layer. You'll be striking your own blow for freedom, while making your point in a manner which it would be impossible to mistake.

On the other hand, a high wind near Jamaica can have its disadvantages. Our hero David Niven found this out as a young man in Bermuda:

> We were never out of the water and became burned the colour of mahogany. I fell slightly in love with a dark-haired beauty of eighteen from Richmond, Virginia. She wore a camellia in her hair on the night I took her for a romantic drive in the full moon. Joe Benevides, though himself the soul of tact on these occasions, sitting bolt upright in his box (of the horse-drawn carriage) and staring ahead oblivious to what was going on behind him, had unknowingly sabotaged my very delicate preliminary moves by feeding his horse some wet grass. It is quite impossible to impress a beautiful girl with your sincerity if your carefully worded murmurings into a shell pink ear have to compete with a barrage of farts.

SHRINKING MUSHROOMS

Rowan Philp of the *Sunday Times* wrote an engaging piece on August 22 1999 about the oyster mushrooms being grown and harvested by former miners down an old water tunnel in the Big Hole in Kimberley. De Beers shaft supervisor Alex Holder is quoted as saying:

There's only one thing about them the miners don't like – they told us these mushrooms are so sensitive you can't even break wind around them.

HISTORY'S MOST EMBARRASSING MOMENT

In his exquisitely entertaining *Brief Lives* the seventeenth century biographer John Aubrey tells the sad story of Edward de Vere, seventeenth Earl of Oxford (1550-1604):

> This Earle of Oxford, making of his law obeisance to Queen Elizabeth, happened to let a Fart, at which he was so abashed and ashamed that he went to Travell, 7 yeares. On his returne the Queen welcomed him home, and sayd, My Lord, I had forgott the Fart.

Since many people believe de Vere wrote the plays of Shakespeare, this might be one of the most significant events in literary history, and all of Shakespeare's plays might have to be reinterpreted in this light.

METHANE MAYHEM

A raging academic controversy over human methane blew up a few Christmases ago when Australian gasto-enterologist Terry Bolin of Sydney's Prince of Wales Hospital urged people to avoid flatulence-producing turkey and plum pudding to help save the ozone layer. The average person emitted a litre a day, he said.

Professor Rodney Taylor of the British Digestive Foundation then pointed out that methane was produced by a high-fibre diet and that vegetarians were more likely to add to the methane crisis. 'Just to put it into perspective, the average cow produces 500 litres of methane a day.'

Dr Jeremy Leggett of Greenpeace leapt into the fray with: 'The real dangers of methane lie not with farting Australians' but with bacterial digestive processes which have stored millions of tonnes of methane in frozen bogs under the tundra. 'As the world warms,' he went on, 'these will be released in quantities that will boost global warming and add to ozone depletion.'

Not so, said Professor Tom Wigley of the climate research unit at the University of East Anglia: 'Methane doesn't destroy ozone. Methane increases the amount of ozone. And so the more you fart – if you can get it up there into the stratosphere – the better it is for the ozone layer.

'I did a little calculation on the greenhouse effect of extra farts over Christmas. If a billion people – which is about the Christian world – fart an extra two litres of methane a day for seven days over Christmas, that would produce one hundred of a teragram of methane (a million grams). That's quite a lot of methane. But present emissions are about 500 teragrams so we are talking about an increment of only one fifty-thousandth. The temperature effect would be about a hundred-thousandth of a degree Celsius.

'From a climate point of view, don't worry about farting. For the ozone layer, fart as much as you possibly can.'

So there you are, gentle reader. Feel free to indulge in your Christmas dinner in the comfortable knowledge that you are improving the ozone layer, if not the festive atmosphere around you.

(We are indebted to Tim Radford's *High Wind* for the above)

To end the wind section, here are two more sure-fire cures from Abbot Feckenham's *Book of sovereigne medicines against the most common and knowne diseases* (all three were quoted by Mollie Harris in *Privies Galore)*:

FOR BELLIE TROBLED WITH WYNDE, GAPYNES OR GNAWINGS:

Take culver donnge, brayed finelie and sodd in a pynte of white wyne, and uppon a clean cloathe laye it playster weise uppon yr bellie and it shall expell the wynde and payne thereof.

('culver' – the old word for pigeon or dove;
'bray' – to pound into a powder, as in a mortar;
'sodd' – cook by boiling)

FOR THE SAME:

Take a good quanteitie of plantyne leaves and beinge verye well sodd, put it into a close stoole, and sit thereon, that maieste receive the ayre thereof uppward into thy bodye and it takethe away the payne of the bellie incontinent.

('close stoole' – a commode)

37

HONORÉ DE BALZAC:

I should like one of these days to be so well known, so popular, so celebrated, so famous, that it would permit me to break wind in society, and society would think it a most natural thing.

NEWS FLASH !

Dinosaur fans may like to know that there is a mechanical triceratops called Cera in Universal's Islands of Adventure theme park in Orlando, Florida, that allows children to pet her – and will pee and fart on cue.

ANSWER TO QUESTION ON PAGE 21

The Expedition of Humphry Clinker by Tobias Smollett, published in 1771. Mr Bramble, in the opening words of the book, writes to his doctor with his concerns:

'The pills are good for nothing; I might as well swallow snowballs to cool my veins. I have told you over and over, how hard I am to move; and at this time of day, I ought to know something of my own constitution.'

'I had a loo in Africa...'

NOSTALGIA
(JENNY)

Nostalgia is looking back with affection. Ace scriptwriter John Cundill (long lost to Australia) wrote a spot-on piece in the August 1984 *Style* called *When Did You Last Pull the Chain?*

> How many familiar, everyday things we've taken for granted as part of our lives are slipping away unnoticed into obsolescence? The manual typewriter? The dial telephone? The hot water bottle? The safety razor? Carbolic soap? White tennis balls? ... Knitted socks? Darned socks? The doiley? Boiled sweets? The bathing cap? The button-up fly? Hair oil? Castor oil? Brooklax? Men's hats? The tie-pin? ... 'Short back and sides'? ...
>
> When last did you actually pull the chain? Now there's a link with the past! I had occasion to recently. Clunk, swish, gurgle – and the memories came swirling back.

In my grandfather's gracious old Pietermaritzburg home the lavatory was one of those spacious Edwardian temples of sanitation. It had a floor of geometric black and tan tiles, a generous wooden seat, a high-rise cistern and a panelled door with a fanlight that faced on to a tranquil courtyard with doves cooing in the monkey-puzzle tree. Leaning against the walls were knee-deep piles of *National Geographics* which made it a place not only of peaceful contemplation but of entertainment and learning.

However, the peace evaporated when you finished your business and got up. Being of a scientific bent (he discovered a technique for making a solid extract from wattle bark which provided the tannin used in the curing of leather), Grandpa had installed an automatic flushing system: as you rose, the seat rose with you and the cistern dispensed a mighty rush of water that would have shamed Niagara. My youngest brother was so terrified of Grandpa's thunderbox that he refused to venture in without a chaperone.

I had a different terror when I was small. After being snatched away from a close encounter with a puffadder, I was afraid of snakes and became convinced that they could swim up through the S-bend and bite me on the bum. My mother pooh-poohed the idea vigorously and because she was a registered nurse and therefore an authority on matters of hygiene, the horrid image faded with time. Now it seems that my fears weren't so far-fetched after all...

> The Cape Cobra has a curiously disconcerting habit that could quite literally scare the pants off you: it slithers indoors in search of water, sometimes seeking refuge under the rim of a toilet seat! This has been known to happen in the environs of Cape Town, where the snakes come down into gardens on the slopes of the Twelve Apostles.
>
> Their quest for water often ends at a fishpond or a dripping tap; but in the absence of these, the snakes sometimes find their way into a house where they may slake their thirst in a toilet bowl.
>
> From *Reader's Digest - Southern African Wildlife*

Even worse, my cousin Shirley Grindley who has been living and working in McBride's Camp in the Timbavati, wrote in her last Christmas letter:

> We have also had some exciting encounters with an Egyptian cobra whose territory appears to overlap significantly with ours.
>
> One fateful night I bumbled into the bathroom with my tiny torch just in time to see the cobra, hood extended, emerging from the loo! It was the most unreal sight I have ever seen and it flashed through my mind that it looked like an art deco painting – very elegant but also rather decadent.

Fortunately the combination of the light and my shout to Roy frightened it and it disappeared back down the pipe in a swirl of water. It has made going to the loo quite an adventure ever since.

KIDS AND LAVS

Clive James, the Australian critic and TV personality, has written a warm, funny autobiography called *Unreliable Memoirs* that has many echoes for South Africans. His earliest days at school were traumatic:

> The only thing I liked about school was skipping around in circles until the music stopped, then lying down on the floor for Quiet Time. I was very good at Quiet Time. Otherwise it was all a bit hopeless. I piddled on the floor when it was my turn to sing. Conversely, I got caught drinking my daily bottle of milk in the lavatory. For some reason this was regarded as a fearful crime.

After a mishap when he and his mother missed each other after school, the headmistress commented at the next morning assembly:

> 'Ah yes, that's the little boy who ran away from his mother.' Thanks a lot, witch. I kacked my pants on the spot.
> The whole secret of kacking your pants, incidentally, is to produce a rock-solid blob which will slide down your leg in one piece and can be rolled away into hiding at the point of the toe. That way, your moment of shame can be kept to the proportions of a strictly local disaster. But if you

let go with anything soft, it takes two teachers to clean you up and the whole affair attracts nationwide publicity.

Our youngest daughter went through a period of dropping her tiny knickers in the lavatory and flushing them away to roars of laughter – causing serious constipation in the septic tank. Prince William seems to have had the same idea. In March 1984 the *Daily Mail* reported:

A ROYAL FLUSH FROM WILLIAM

Still three months short of his second birthday, Prince William has become a leading exponent of our throw-away society.

From Kensington Palace the latest news is that his favourite trick is to flush his possessions down the loo.

Apparently William dislikes his footwear the most and several pairs of his shoes were disposed of in this manner before Nanny Barbara Barnes, 40, was able to intercept the lad, who is intrigued by the flushing process. Even Prince Charles has not escaped his heir's mischievousness – William has deposited a pair of his hand-made shoes in the bowl and was somewhat surprised when they did not disappear with the ease with which his bootees do...

The princeling is not yet aware that he will be joined later this year by a sister or a brother and it will be interesting to see how he reacts to losing some of the limelight. Perhaps the royal plumber will be put on permanent standby.

Happy memories of lavatories past are shared by two Englishwomen who both became writers. Gwen Raverat's memoir *Period Piece* dwelt with great affection on her grandfather Charles Darwin's home:

> And just as everything else at Down was perfect, so there too was the most beautiful, secret, romantic lavatory that ever was known; at the end of a long passage and up several steps. It had the only window which looked out over the orchard, and was always full of a dim green light. You looked down into the tops of the apple trees; and when I read Romeo & Juliet ... the line 'That tips with silver all these fruit-tree tops' always made me think of that window.

Agatha Christie was equally enthralled by the atmosphere of a grand WC:

> Ealing ... had all the romance of a foreign country. One of its principal joys was its lavatory. It had a splendidly large mahogany lavatory seat. Sitting on it one felt exactly like a Queen on her throne, and I rapidly translated Dicksmistress (herself) into Queen Marguerite, and Dickie (her canary) became her son, Prince Goldie, the heir to the throne. He sat at her right hand on the small circle which enclosed the handsome Wedgwood plug handle. Here in the morning I would retreat, sit bowing, giving audience, and extending my hand to be kissed until summoned angrily to come out by others wishing to enter.

Roald Dahl had far less pleasant memories of his time as a fag at Repton, which he wrote about in his autobiography *Boy*. (The 'Boazers' he talks about were prefects).

> 'Go and heat my seat in the bogs,' Wilberforce said. 'I want it warm.'
>   I hadn't the faintest idea what any of this meant, but I already knew better than to ask questions of a Boazer. I hurried away and found a fellow Fag

who told me the meaning of this curious order.

It meant that the Boazer wished to use the lavatory but that he wanted the seat warmed for him before he sat down. The six House lavatories, none with doors, were situated in an unheated outhouse and on a cold day in winter you could get frostbite out there if you stayed too long. This particular day was icy-cold, and I went out through the snow into the outhouse and entered number one lavatory, which I knew was reserved for Boazers only.

I wiped the frost off the seat with my handkerchief, then I lowered my trousers and sat down. I was there a full fifteen minutes in the freezing cold before Wilberforce arrived on the scene.

'Have you got the ice off it?' he asked.

'Yes, Wilberforce.'

'Is it warm?'

'It's as warm as I can get it, Wilberforce,' I said.

'We shall soon find out,' he said. 'You can get off now.'

I got off the lavatory seat and pulled up my trousers. Wilberforce lowered his own trousers and sat down. 'Very good,' he said. 'Very good indeed.' He was like a winetaster sampling an old claret. 'I shall put you on my list,' he added.

I stood there doing up my fly-buttons and not knowing what on earth he meant.

'Some Fags have cold bottoms,' he said, 'and some have hot ones. I only use hot-bottomed Fags to heat my bog-seat. I won't forget you.'

Schoolboys have other uses. The Thomas Cobbleigh column in the *Sunday Times* of 13 March 1994 ended with the following:

Cobbleigh has no doubt that every woman reader of this column would wish to nominate UK schoolboy Lee Jones as Son of the Month, possibly even the Millennium.

When Lee's mum Sheila, 40, got jammed in a window he wanted her to look her best when firemen came to the rescue. So the 13-year-old lad combed her hair, powdered her nose and sprayed on perfume.

Sheila got stuck halfway when she tried to clamber out of a friend's loo window in Saundersfoot, Wales, after locking herself in.

TWO LITTLE LOO STORIES

Joey, aged two, is sitting with legs swinging and hands clutching the toilet seat.

'What are those for?' pointing to a pile of magazines.

'People who like to read on the lav,' says Granny.

'But how can they when they have to hold on?'

(From *The Star*, 1 October 1984)

Joey was right to be cautious. In May 1990, it took six London firemen to cut through a toilet seat to free Kerry Anne Davis, aged three, who had slipped backwards and got stuck with her legs in the air.

POTTIES

In the days when the long-drop was out in the back yard, and even after the newfangled flush toilet had crept up on to the back veranda, posh houses had bedside cupboards (sometimes zinc-lined) that concealed chamber pots for use during the night. The rest had to make do with a potty under the bed.

Jenny writes:

I am of the generation who had maiden aunts in the family – many of them bereft of boyfriends or fiancés or simply a choice of men by the devastating losses of the First World War. After the Second World War, things were very different: marriage was no longer the Major Undertaking it had been, divorce became common, living together became acceptable, gay women came out of the closet – and spinsters and maiden aunts faded from the scene.

My two doughty great-aunts were by no means shy and retiring. Barely out of school, Aunt Marjorie drove ambulances in France during the first war (for which she was awarded the MBE), ran her own hotel in London for decades, sat up on roof-tops as a fire warden during the second war, and had a number of distinguished lovers. Aunt Shirley had china blue eyes, a passion for history and farming, and a fine way with words. The Jersey bull on her South Coast dairy farm was called Dashing Daring Dauntless Desmond. She travelled alone on mail trains at ungodly hours and told riveting stories from a fund that never ran dry.

It was a privilege to know them both and to listen to their always stimulating conversation; their intelligence, independence and spirited lives made them wonderful role models.

But when they came to stay, you had to provide a potty under the bed. They had grown up on an Estcourt farm where night visits to the long-drop were out of the question, and they had got used to using chamber pots. For years the Aunts' potty reposed in the family bathroom cupboard, ready for the next visit: a white porcelain receptacle with a curly handle and a raised design and a transfer of pink roses on the front. After they died and it was given to me, I couldn't bring myself to install it on the windowsill with a resident pot plant. It wasn't out of delicacy. It was because that potty was an icon of a seemly privacy that has faded today, along with maiden aunts. I gave it away to a cousin.

> Letter to *The Times* from Mrs Sheila P Hart, 28 August 1991:
> Sir, 'Where have all the chamber pots gone? Gone to be flower pots every one.'

A POTTIED HISTORY

Lucinda Lambton is an English professional photographer specialising in architecture. Her *Temples of Convenience*, first published in 1978 and now available in a beautiful Pavilion edition, is the ultimate reference book for lavatory aficionados, both for its detailed historical introduction and for its breathtaking photographs of loos ancient and modern, humble and grand. She says of Roman potties:

> There were no latrines or privies attached to houses. Basins and pots were used, looked after by slaves employed exclusively for the tempting tasks. 'When a gentleman wanted his chamber-pot,' wrote Petronius, '...it was a common way of speaking to make a noise with the finger and thumb, by snapping them together...'
>
> The luxuriant depravity of the Romans reached its peak with chamber-pots, and other such vessels, being made of rare stones and metals. 'It would

have been well for the Romans,' wrote Rollestone in 1751, 'if they had but remained contented with earthen jurdens – we may date the commencement of (their) ruin from the introduction of gold and silver chamber-pots and close-stool pans.'

From Jeremy Beadle's *Today's the Day! A Chronicle of the Curious*

August 13, 1889: A breakthrough in chamber pots was patented in England. Its object was, 'To obviate the necessity for putting the thumb inside the vessel when holding the same, as is now generally the custom.'

Nearly two thousand years after the Romans, potties remained integral to Indian bathrooms and were still being emptied by servants who were little better than slaves. John Masters, born into a family that had served in India since 1805, became a Colonel in the old Indian Army, then turned to writing when he retired. His novels (nearly all bestsellers, though quite dated now) range across the British experience in India. In *Bugles & A Tiger*, the first volume of his autobiography, he explained:

A ghuslkhana corresponds in function to a bathroom, but it is a profound misconception to think of white porcelain, taps, or water sanitation. The ghuslkhana is small and square and has a hole in the outer wall to let out water and let in snakes. One corner, around that outlet, is fenced in by a low parapet the height of a single brick. In this enclosure sits an oval zinc tub.

Outside the parapet is a slatted wooden board to stand on, and a jug; a chamber pot; a packet of Bromo hanging from a nail; and a wooden thing on four legs whose proper name may possibly be 'toilet', but which was never called anything but 'the thunderbox'. The thunderbox has a hole in the middle of the seat, and a hinged top. Under the hole, fitted into the structure, is a deep enamel pot called a top hat...

When a sahib (has finished) ... he shouts, 'Mehtar!' into the empty air, and forgets all about it. The sweeper, who spends his day dozing on his heels and smoking bidis within earshot of his life's work, comes, removes the top hat, cleans it out with a broom and by hand into a pit or a burning-oven, and returns it to its place.

POTTY PRANKS AND TABOOS

The receptacle that served our grandparents and great-aunts came in either decorative white porcelain (as described above) or more utilitarian white or green enamel rimmed in navy blue. Today it has evolved into a jolly plastic potty with a sturdy base and sometimes even a musical accompaniment. Recently an American woman designed an encouraging variation that should go down well with the two-year-old set. In December 1998 Universal Press Syndicate reported:

Laurita Bledsoe of Detroit in the US was recently granted a patent for her Talking Potty trainer, which fits over a toilet and houses computer sound chips, a tape player and speakers to give applause and verbal feedback for jobs well done.

Another American starter toilet has a microchip that plays *Little Brown Jug* and *Mary Had a Little Lamb* when its gold-plated electronic sensor detects moisture in the bowl. It's called the Hop On! Musical Potty.

Enamel potties were a favourite prop of students' antics in earlier days – either worn at a rakish angle on the head or placed after a dangerous drunken climb on top of the nearest flagpole, statue or building summit. Queen Victoria, who poses regally outside the old red-brick Supreme Court building in Pietermaritzburg with her orb and sceptre, was frequently given a potty to hold as well.

Elevated potties were nothing new, of course. Robert Graves, speculating on what a future historian would conclude about twentieth century customs, wrote tongue in cheek in *Occupation Writer*:

Shortly before the 'Great War for Civilisation' ... there was a student at Oxford University famous for his 'practical joking' and for deriding the most sacred taboos of his time. It was he who first defiled a local altar, 'The Martyrs' Memorial', by climbing to its very summit at night-time and planting a chamber-pot – a stringently tabooed vessel – on the cross that crowned it. The civic authorities had great difficulty in removing this scandalous object, because climbing the Memorial was no easy feat, and the chamber-pot, being made of enamel-ware rather than, as was first thought, of porcelain, could not be dislodged by rifle fire.

An interesting theory on taboos was put forward by Professor Randolph Quirk, vice-chancellor of the University of London in 1983, in a book of essays called *Style and Communication in the English Language*. Michael Leapman of the *Daily Express* reported him as saying that:

Filthy language, formerly regarded as a masculine speciality, is the latest bastion of privilege that women have successfully stormed...

Why do people swear anyway? Dr Quirk says it is mainly to do with the thrill of breaking taboos. Man, he says, is the only species that has such taboos, mostly stemming from our unwillingness to perform the lavatorial functions in public. The free use of dirty language is, in one sense, a substitute for defecating in the open...

So next time you are out to dinner and you ask a woman politely to pass the salt, do not be surprised or offended if you are told to blankety-blank fetch it yourself. Remember that she is only trying to introduce a feeling of comradeship, to share the illicit thrill of breaking a taboo. Try telling her to naff off.

Before we leave the subject, here is an item from the late lamented South African *Sunday Express* about someone who had a unique problem. This winning vignette by Stephen Davimes appeared on August 5 1984:

DRIVEN POTTY (10 000 TIMES OVER)

Recently I was running my eye over some newspaper smalls when I noticed under the miscellaneous sales section: '10 000 chamber pots for sale'... Why would anyone be wanting to sell 10 000 potties? ...So I dialled the number at the bottom of the ad.

It turned out that someone had added a zero to an order of 1 000 plastic chamber pots. Explained an Xactics Plastics company spokesman – who would only give his name as a Mr Enzo – that the company now had a massive problem.

'Computers don't make mistakes but programmers do. Our production is controlled by computer and someone somewhere must have added a zero to an order.' Now they're stored out in the veld in large containers – going to pot. Anyone who wants them can have them at R1 apiece. Or you can make an offer for a quantity. A job-lot...

And what do they look like? They're small and they're white, every last one of them. These days potties come in all colours, shapes and sizes, costing from R3 upwards. The plain potties may prove difficult to move.

Perhaps they could be used as flower pots? Pot plants? Perhaps a well-known brewery firm could give away one free with every case of beer, suggests Mr Enzo...

Now there's a suggestion for your next promotion, SAB. You could ensure the loyalty of a whole new generation of students by providing each with a suitably emblazoned receptacle for silly pranks.

AN EIGHTEENTH CENTURY
DITTY

Presumptious pisse-pot how
didst thou offend?
Compelling females on their
hams to bend?
To kings and Queens we
humbly bend the knee,
But Queens themselves are
forced to stoop to thee.

– *Scatological Rites*

COMMODES

The commode, a chair with a round hole in the seat and a receptacle that slides in and out, is still in use at the bedsides of the infirm; no longer the cumbersome wooden throne our great-grandmothers used but an efficient, light, streamlined nursing aid.

There is a lovely story in Jeremy Beadle's *Today's the Day!* about a Pope's throne with a hidden agenda. On January 23 1294:

Naughty Pope Boniface VIII was confirmed in his holy calling in a bizarre ceremony which took place outside the Lateran Palace. He was ensconced in an ancient throne of red marble, which had originally come from the city's public baths. It had a seat with a hole in it, and looked suspiciously like a commode.

Some said that's exactly what it was, and that the Pope's sitting on it was a gesture of self-abasement. Others believed it had a more scientific purpose, and was in fact used to facilitate a physical examination of the Pontiff, so there would never be a second pope-in-drag like the infamous 'Pope Joan'.

They needn't have worried. Boniface was a healthy man, with a healthy sex life. He saw sexuality as no sin and added that going to bed with 'women and boys' was no more than rubbing one hand against the other.

BEDPANS

Bedpans are also still with us: unchanged in shape and as uncomfortable and ornery as ever.

THE BED-PAN AND I

(from *How to Enjoy Your Operation* by Vivian Ellis)

This is not for the squeamish. It describes a patient's fight to overcome an almost insuperable object of elliptical design... This object is never mentioned in drawing rooms or diplomatic soirées. Surprisingly, it is seldom referred to in modern novels, where hardly any bodily function goes unnoticed. Perhaps this is because with the exception of our intrepid nurses, who juggle with them like plates, people are more afraid of bed-pans than atom bombs...

This instrument of torture was designed by some incompetent fiend in order to alleviate the lot of a sufferer who is bedridden. He would be far better off dead on a wheeled commode. Instead of relief, it increases discomfort to an alarming degree and for the following reasons:

<u>One</u>. If the patient is at all sensitive, he feels as ridiculous as a red-capped pixie perched on a toadstool in a suburban front garden.

<u>Two</u>. Unless he is what is known as well upholstered, the patient is almost certain to receive a sharp jab in the buttocks every time he is deposited upon the rack.

<u>Three</u>. He will soon discover that the receptacle is so designed as to be insufficiently deep for the purpose for which it was presumably invented.

Moreover, it really requires a mounting block. The average bed-pan is as difficult to mount as a two-humped Bactrian camel – whose temperament it much resembles.

POSTSCRIPT

Dean Swift was a fastidious man who described in his *Directions to Servants*, 1745, a good ploy for embarrassing insensitive employers:

> I am very much offended with those Ladies, who are so proud and lazy, that they will not be at pains of stepping into the garden to pluck a rose, but keep an odious implement, sometimes in the bedchamber itself, or at least in a dark closet adjoining, which they make use of to ease their worst necessities; and you are the usual carriers away of the pan which, maketh not only the chamber, but even their clothes offensive, to all who come near. Now, to cure them of this odious practice, let me advise you, on whom this office lieth, to convey away this utensil, that you will do it openly, down the great stairs, and in the presence of the footmen; and, if anybody knocketh, to open the street door, while you have the vessel in your hands: this, if anything can, will make your lady take the pains of evacuating her person in the proper place, rather than expose her filthiness to all the men servants of the house.

LONG-DROPS

Long-drops, or pit latrines, are not a South African phenomenon (though the name is). The most famous lavatory book in the world, and what must be its shortest bestseller at 30 pages and 3 000 words, was written about long-drops by an American vaudeville artist in 1929.

Chic Sale's forte was an act in which he used the voice of Lem Putt, an imaginary carpenter with a walrus moustache who specialised in building outhouses. Lem's droll instructions as to placing, construction and appurtenances were such a hit with his audiences that Chic wrote them down and, with two friends, published them as *The Specialist*. It was translated into ten languages and within 25 years had sold a million copies in the United States alone – and has never been out of print since.

The English edition of *The Specialist*, a fixture in many South African lavatories over the decades, was published by Putnams and illustrated with woodcuts by the aptly named William Kermode. If you find a copy, treasure it. George Bernard Shaw called it a 'pioneering masterpiece' though another critic of the time, Sir Desmond MacCarthy, sniffed, 'I don't believe that it will amuse the frivolous elect enough, while the jolly, coarse, crude public hardly exists at all in England.'

The myriad fans of Billy Connolly prove otherwise.

Some long-drops have had a certain charm: scrubbed pine seats, daddy-long-legses dancing in the cobwebs, piles of *Farmer's Weeklies*, blades of sunlight slicing through split poles and the unhurried atmosphere of drowsy farm afternoons, redolent of gum trees. The faint aroma of creosote and the stronger bass note of the seething cesspit below added spice to the occasion.

But they were outnumbered by the threatening long-drops, one of which Jenny wrote about in her novel *Thoughts in a Makeshift Mortuary*. The speaker is Jake van Vuuren, a poet:

> 'It stood by itself across the yard like a corrugated-
> iron coffin up on end, with a rotten wooden door

with rusty hinges that screamed like it was in agony every time anyone went in. Inside, it was dark and scary. Cobwebs would drag against your face and there'd be soft sounds of spiders scuttling into cracks. The toilet paper was torn-up squares of newspaper pushed on to a wire hook. The stink in there would stay in your nose long after you came out, no matter how much Jeyes Fluid Ouma used to clean it. For a kid, climbing up on the wooden bench was terrifying. You had to drop your broeks and sit down quick so as not to look down the hole into the blackness, though your eyes were always pulled to it.'

He shivered, even in the cafeteria's fuggy warmth. 'The hole was grown-up sized, much too big for a skinny little backside like mine. You had to sit with your arms out stiff on both sides to prop yourself up, and be quick about your business before they started to shake. I had nightmares about falling through and drowning in that terrible pit, with only the bluebottle flies buzzing round my shit-covered head as witness. And I really believed the kid next door who told me that there was a nest of snakes living down there that could rear up and bite me, this trembling little bum hanging over the void.'

GETTING DOWN TO BASICS

Cesspit drownings are not uncommon (see HORROR STORIES), specially in Africa where pits and septic tanks are often roofed with corrugated iron which inevitably rots. However, long-drops are not as insanitary as they sound and have served us well for centuries.

The basic principle of decomposition is simple, and applies to septic tanks as well as cesspits. According to the indispensable *Handbook for Farmers in South Africa*:

> ...the solid substances sink to the bottom. The anaerobic or air-shunning bacteria in the tank (or pit) immediately begin to attack the solid particles which rise to the surface as a result of the bubbles of gas which are generated around them. Here the gas escapes and the particles sink to the bottom again where they are attacked once more by the bacteria. This process continues until the digestible solids have been completely decomposed and assume the form of a froth.

The traditional way of encouraging bacteria and other useful agents of decomposition is recorded in Mike Nicol's fine historical satire, *This Day & Age*:

> Ma-Fatsoen, dressed to the nines ... waved to Fat Eddie on the verandah dunking dough cakes into his coffee, and, hair shining with rain, disappeared towards the long-drops carrying a sheep's head... (which she drops into the latrine pit)
>
> Some time later the sheep's head stared malignantly up at P. T. George's English arse as he made himself comfortable on the wooden seat. It stared balefully up at the voiding of leg of lamb, mutton chop, mint sauce, spare-rib. Not once did it blare or blink an eye. Above it, a now relieved P T George, feeling he was being watched, kicked closed the door he'd left open to the wet fields. But the feeling persisted, disturbed those precious first moments of his day when he liked to think.

Increasingly uneasy, he stared down through the smell into the pit. The sheep's head glared back.

Fat Eddie was still at breakfast on the verandah when P. T. George, wearing only a shirt and boots, clutching his trousers, came running among the mission cottages, causing children to giggle, men to forget their hangovers, women to shut their eyes, raced across the square and disappeared like a white bob-tail into Pastor Melksop's house, shouting about a dead man in the privy. No it's not, everyone laughed. But no amount of persuading – It's just there for the worms – would take him back to the long-drops, and three days later he left the mission as constipated as a pregnant cat.

One reason why simple earth cesspits work well in Africa is the heat, which encourages rapid decomposition. In cooler northern climates they don't work so well and have to be regularly cleaned out. Mary Queen of Scots wrote to a friend during her imprisonment in Tutbury Castle:

> As no house, with so many low bred people in it as this, can be long kept clean, however orderly they may be, so this house, and I blush to have to say it, wanting proper conveniences for the necessity of nature, has a sickening stench ever lingering in it. On every Saturday too, the cesspools must be cleared out, even to the one below my windows, whence come none of the perfumes of Arabia.

Improved design has produced a new kind of long-drop called the Blair or Ventilated Improved Pit (VIP) toilet, first developed in Zimbabwe, which is slowly spreading to rural areas in Southern Africa (see THE SERIOUS SECTION).

CHLDHOOD MEMORIES BY DAY...

One of Jenny's oldest friends, Ann Snaddon, writes of her farm childhood:

> I have fond memories of the up-the-hill long-drop on our farm below Majuba in Natal. It stood next to the railway line and had a wide wooden seat where I would perch nervously, listening intently so as to gauge the tone of the drone of the up-rising bees beneath the seat (they had a nest there), ready to leap if the note rose too high. The door of the long-drop never shut properly so when the bees were quiet you could sit and watch the trains puff by, counting the trucks and kicking your feet to the click of the wheels on the rails.

Dirk Bogarde also had potent memories of the family long-drop in England. This is from his autobiographical *A Postillion Struck by Lightning:*

The privy had no door, so you just sat there and looked into the ivy; no one could see you through it, but you could see them coming along the little path and so you were able to shout out and tell them not to in time. It was really quite useful. And better than a door really, because that made it rather dark and a bit nasty inside...

There were three seats, like the Bears'. A little low one, a medium one, and the grown-up one. The wood was white and shining where we used to scrub it, and the knots were all hard and sticking up. No one ever used the smallest one, we had the paper and old comics and catalogues for reading in that; and the medium one just had a new tin bucket in it with matches and candles for the candlestick which stood on a bracket by the paper roll, and a cardboard tin of pink carbolic. There were lids to all the seats, with wooden handles, and they had to be scrubbed too...

Sociable two- and three-holers were a feature of early long-drops. Mollie Harris writes in *Privies Galore:*

When we were young we often used to go down to our two-holer with brothers and sisters, and even the next-door neighbour's children. And it wasn't always just for 'business'. Oh, no! You lingered there for ages, to chat and giggle perhaps about a local boy who you fancied. And the smell that was always prevalent never seemed to bother us at all...

On the other hand, if you could sneak down there on your own, it was lovely, away from the crowded cottage. You could just sit there, with the door three parts open, and the sun shining on your legs – to read from the squares of newspaper (the 'bumfodder' as we called it)...or dream or have a quiet cry in secret.

Tranquillity is a long-lost component of our daily lives. Here is Willem Steenkamp in his 'Please don't quote me' column in the *Cape Times* of 15 August 1985:

PRIVY COUNCIL

I grew up at the tail-end, as it were, of the outhouse era in the platteland, and attending to one's needs was an interesting cross-cultural experience for one who had been weaned on the invention of the immortal Crapper.

Some city slickers could not handle it, but the experience was not as terrible as various squeamish souls would have one believe. Even in bad examples of the art one's olfactory nerves usually went into shock within a minute or so, and I personally never had any trouble with snakes, scorpions, tarantulas or any of the other beasts which are said to lurk under the seat.

It is also true that on a pleasant day, once one's nose had gone numb, an old-fashioned 'kleinhuisie' or privy was a good place for contemplation. Or maybe that was all an illusion created by the fact that one's brain-cells had been struck down along with one's smelling apparatus.

Writing in the *Observer* on 6 April 1980, Michael Denny had mixed memories of a Cornish long-drop that had just been replaced:

ALL I WANTED FOR EASTER WAS MY INSIDE LOO

To get to the outside loo you go out through the new french windows that haven't got a latch yet and jam shut in wet weather ... over the pile of rubble in the ex-conservatory ... round the corner, past the dripping nettles ... down the steep narrow slippery path where you have to bend down under the brambles that somehow never get cut, and there you are... Once I felt a damp, sliding sensation on my foot. It was a long brown inquisitive slug.

But there are compensations. Once you get there our outside loo is a nice place, stone-built with a good Delabole slate roof and a fine view of our big old box tree. There are the pleasant rural sounds of cows, gulls, gales, etc, and in the autumn the chance of finding good nuts on the path from the hazel tree that hangs over the roof.

... AND BY NIGHT

Long-drops at night are a different experience entirely. Michael Denny explained that he had finally opted for inside comfort because:

> I got fed up with forever emptying children's potties and wiping up the attendant ongoing mess and taking my elder daughter over the rubble and past the nettles to the loo because she's frightened of the dark.

And Ann Snaddon has fearful memories of night visits to the long-drop:

> Down that hole I remember losing many things: torches, hankies, whole rolls of toilet paper, a bag once, marbles, *Farmer's Weeklies* and *Reader's Digests*. But the worst were the torches, because as the light gurgled down to its dark doom, you were left in inky blackness to grope your way back round the store house, past the fowl hok, down some badly spaced stepping stones, over a gutter and into the back yard, convinced that the bog house ghoul was after you.

Though Dirk Bogarde enjoyed nocturnal visits:

> Sometimes at night it was rather nice to go there down the path in the dark, with the candle guttering in the candlestick, and shadows leaping and fluttering all around and the ivy glossy where the golden light caught it. Sometimes little beady eyes gleamed in at you and vanished; and you could hear scurrying sounds and the tiny squeaks of voles and mice.

And who could forget the lovely passage in André Brink's *An Act of Terror* where a small boy rushes inside to call his older sister...

> 'Maria! Maria, come, look, there's an angel in the outhouse.' You'd found it, you explained, near the back door, while you were peeing: a small creature lighting up the night. You'd followed it this way and that through the back yard, into the outhouse. A firefly, I guessed. But you were adamant. It was an angel. Keeping a straight face, I went outside with you to have a look, but the deep well below the round hole in the outhouse was pitch-dark. No sign of angels...
>
> At supper the following evening you asked, 'What kind of food do angels eat?' ...
>
> It was Mum who said in her quiet way, as if it was the most natural thing in the world, 'Sugar water. Angels drink nothing but sugar water.'
>
> ...an hour later I heard you go out again, as usual, for your evening pee; and once again you stayed out very long. And because I knew how scared you were of the dark, I went out to look for you. And found you. Sitting hunched up on the

wooden seat in the outhouse, the torch beside you, staring into the hole.

The light made a huge black shadow on the corrugated iron wall.

I remember every detail of the scene. The open door with the uneven heart-shape sawn into it (Dad's brave but unconvincing handiwork). The long nail holding squares of newsprint. The cardboard box with old copies of magazines. The smell of Jeyes Fluid. And you crouching there, staring into the malodorous darkness, a saucer of sugar water in your hand.

THE BUCKET SYSTEM

The bucket system was one step up from a long-drop and lasted until the Fifties in the older parts of our cities before being superseded by septic tanks and water-borne sewerage. Brixton and Parkview in Johannesburg still have a network of sanitary lanes where the night-soil carts did their weekly rounds.

Bucket toilets were common in the Commonwealth, including Australia where outhouses are still called 'dunnies'. Clive James wrote of the Sydney dunny men in his hilarious *Unreliable Memoirs*:

Ever since I could remember, the dunny man had come running down the driveway once a week. From inside the house, we could hear his running footsteps. Then we could hear the rattle and thump as he lifted the lavatory, took out the full pan, clipped on a special lid, and set down an empty pan in its place. After more rattling and banging, there was an audible intake of breath as he hefted the full pan on to his shoulder. Then the footsteps went back along the driveway, slower this time but still running. From outside in the street there was rattling, banging and shouting as the full pan was loaded on to the dunny cart along with all the other full pans.

I often watched the dunny cart from the front window. As it slowly made its noisome way down the street, the dunny men ran to and from it with awesome expertise. They wore shorts, sandshoes, and nothing else except a sun-tan suspiciously deep on the forearms. Such occasional glimpses were all one was allowed by one's parents and all that was encouraged even by the dunny men themselves. They preferred to work in nobody's company except their own. They were a band apart.

THE DITCHFIELD SANITARY SYSTEM

The early bucket toilets were improved by the addition of ash hoppers. After each use, the bucket contents were doused with ash which absorbed both smells and liquids. Barry Morton remembers:

> Pinelands Garden City was established in 1924, modelled on the lines of Welwyn Garden City in England. Run by a local management board, it was independent from Cape Town and could not afford water-borne sewage disposal.
>
> Our toilets were outside in the back yard, lit and ventilated by gaps at the top and bottom of the

door. The apparatus was an imposing throne of pale varnished wood formed by two rectangular boxes, the lower being the seat which concealed a large iron bucket. Behind it the other box, about 4½ feet tall, contained a steel hopper hinged and suspended from the top and with a lip at the bottom projecting over the bucket.

The hopper was filled with ash and operated by a chain which emerged from a hole and ended in an elegant white ceramic knob. A notice requested the departing user to 'Close lid and pull chain thrice before leaving.' At each pull the swinging hopper thumped against the inside of the box, dislodging a handful of ash into the bucket.

Once a week a large grey-painted Leyland lorry would arrive with its cheerful crew of men with damp sacks draped over their heads and shoulders. The bottom part of the throne would be removed, the full bucket emptied into a sack and hefted on to the lorry while another man would clean and paint the bucket with a black creosote substance – I suppose it was something like Jeyes Fluid – and a third would fill the hopper with more ash.

This all ended just before World War II when Pinelands with much digging and trenching became connected to the Cape Town sewerage system. I missed going out into the yard in the evening with a candle and a book, just as I missed the daily deliveries of bread in a large basket, the milkman, the egg man who delivered his eggs every week in a Model B Ford tourer, the knife sharpener, the boot repair man on a bicycle, the besom man with his mournful cry selling reed brooms, the fish cart with its driver blowing his 'Snoektown' fish horn, the water cart spraying the roads and the policeman who patrolled the streets at night on his bicycle and would check your house daily when you were away on holiday...

Like Clive James's dunny men, the bucket men were a band apart, said to come from a particular tribe. Did they move on to another speciality like the other entrepreneurs who once plied their trades in Pinelands, or were they too swept away by the overwhelming tidal wave of progress?

SEPTIC TANKS

These remain with us in parts of the country that have graduated from pit latrines but still don't have a sewerage system. The construction of a septic tank is a specialised affair, though most are bought ready-made today like fibreglass pools. Since they have no place in a chapter devoted to long-drops, we will simply offer you a memory of the time when the septic tank at Jenny's Durban home stopped working properly and the corporation's sanitation tanker had to come and slurp it out with a honeysucker: a long flexible ribbed pipe like an elephant's trunk.

The guava tree that grew nearby never had a decent crop again.

OUTHOUSES & LITERATURE

Jeanette Winterson, English novelist: I cannot over-emphasise the importance of an outside toilet when there is no room of one's own.

It was on the lavatory that I first read Freud and DH Lawrence and perhaps, after all, it was the right place. We kept a rubber torch hung on the cistern and I had to juggle my Saturday job money between buying forbidden books and new batteries. It was fairly easy to smuggle books in and out of the house; what was difficult was finding somewhere to keep them. I opted for under the mattress, and anyone with a single bed, standard size, and paperbacks, standard size, will discover that seventy-seven can be comfortably accommodated. But as my collection grew, I began to worry that my mother might notice that her daughter's bed was rising visibly.

One day she did. She burned everything.

Alan Coren: No visit to Dove Cottage, Grasmere, is complete without examining the outhouse where Hazlitt's father, a Unitarian minister of strong liberal views, attempted to put his hand up Dorothy Wordsworth's skirt.

OUTHOUSES & FINE ART

From *The Boston Globe* on 21 January 1985, bylined M R Montgomery and quoted in Mollie Harris's *Privies Galore:*

The art world is buggy over a newly discovered painting by William de Kooning. A breathless agent has announced that the price is beyond estimate...

It is a fairly simple painting on a long rectangle of poplar wood, ... broken by three carved voids in the shape of asymmetrical ovals. The borders of the ovals are carefully smoothed and burnished with the sort of patina one usually sees on the toes of the statues of saints, where the true believers have rubbed the statue for good luck.

Anyone over forty who has ever spent time in a rural environment, or a poorly appointed summer camp, would recognise the object for what it is, and what it is, is: a three-holer...

Mr de Kooning's contribution (the sculptor is unknown) is ... perhaps intended to be humorous. He has simply, sometime before World War II, applied white and black paint to the object with the apparent intention of making it look like marble...

The painting is currently hung horizontally against a vertical wall, which somewhat tends to obscure its true nature, except, of course, to flies.

If a sociable privy seat has made it into the rarefied realm of modern art, can the high temples of convenience be far behind?

MORE FART THAN ART

After giving Van der Merwe a presentation about a timeshare scheme, the agent said: 'Now, Mr Van der Merwe, we'd better discuss the levy.'

'Tell me,' said Van, 'is that an inside levy or an outside levy?'

A Dunny Down Under

PUBLIC
CONVENIENCES

One of the down-sides of progress has been the decline of the public convenience from the grand establishments of old to the utilitarian row of skimpily partitioned and often squalid toilets where one hesitates to sit for fear of contracting a dread disease. Jonathan Glancey put it very well in his article *The Splendour of British Loos Past*:

> Why are modern public lavatories so mean, ugly and, if they work at all, so brutally functional? In Victorian and Edwardian Britain the public lavatory was a public occasion.
>
> The foundation stone ... would be laid by a civic dignitary, the urinals carved from rich Italian marble, pipework forged from brass, stalls divided from one another by sturdy partitioning, floors laid in decorative tiles and cisterns supported by wrought iron brackets...
>
> Then, when functional architecture took over in the 40s, the British public lavatory seemed to take its cue from the Nissen hut. Why this change of attitude? Why, given that the public lavatory is one of the most popular rooms, is it now built of the cheapest possible materials and crammed into the most inconvenient corners?
>
> He concludes that, 'The answer lies in modern attitudes. Genteel folk are embarrassed by the lavatory,' and goes on to say that while new bars and hotels often have superb public lavatories, major public buildings and institutions pale by comparison.

Certainly those of us who remember the spacious and well appointed Ladies' Rest Rooms in select department stores like John Orrs and Stuttafords have reason to mourn. Gone are the mirrors and flowers and padded stools and chintz armchairs where tired shoppers could rest their feet, leaving a grateful tickey in the saucer for the cloakroom attendant with the obsequious smile and her bunions concealed in felt slippers with pompoms. Though the style lingers on in the powder rooms of country clubs, they are only open to members and their guests.

The word 'cloakroom' seem to have disappeared entirely along with usherettes, *African Mirror* and *Stage & Cinema*, though we imagine there are still examples of the genre in our city halls.

From Jeremy Beadle's *Today's the Day! A Chronicle of the Curious.*

February 2 1852: The very first public loo with flushing toilets was opened in London's Fleet Street by, of all people, the Society of Arts. Needless to say, it was a 'Gents' and the ladies had to wait another nine days to get a loo of their very own in Bedford Street. Delicately dubbed 'Public Waiting Rooms', they were tastefully fitted out; the WCs themselves were boxed-in in polished wood and a staff of three made sure everything ran smoothly. The Society published advertisements announcing the conveniences in The Times and handed out 50 000 explanatory leaflets. Unfortunately the idea was abandoned, since by the end of the month only 58 men and 24 women had used the loos. They failed to catch on probably because the Society of Arts charged tuppence for spending a penny.

Modern hotels and cinema complexes may be lavish with marble and stainless steel but the stalls lack a decent privacy, the fixtures are often missing and it takes a major effort to wrench more than two flimsy sheets off the bogroll. Hot-air hand dryers, far from being more hygienic, are now said to harbour more germs than the old roller towels that had inevitably reached their end by the time you needed one, locked in a damp noxious loop used by at least fifty previous pairs of hands. In our more venerable buildings the plumbing and fittings can be so decrepit that you have to beg for a key to a private haven from a snooty receptionist.

Bottom of the rung are the municipal public conveniences built below street level that Jenny's friend Brian Snaddon writes about descending into with:

> ...a dread, ominous feeling ... almost expecting to find Orpheus there adjusting his dress, or the odd sleek nose-twitching sewer rat. Down there, the calming roar of the city street gives way to sepulchral echoes, water-spouts are at work in secret places, doors bang with a boom and there are signs stuck up saying such things as: 'Wash & Brush Up 5c', 'No Loitering' and, in fine print, 'The City Council Accepts No Liability For...'
>
> You reel in, slam yourself into the relative safety of a closet and proceed, the mind buzzing with distaste and alarm. Relief achieved, you discover there is no toilet paper. Gloom and disquiet repossess the soul. How to attract attention – thump on the door, perhaps? Shout, 'Hullo there!' Stick your head up over the door? Stick your belt under the door and flap it? Start singing loudly, or walk out at half mast...'

SANITARY SLEAZE

As intrepid travellers we've been forced to function in far, far worse places: filthy squat lavatories, clogged toilets in aeroplanes, stadium horror-holes awash with urine. The fastidious used to line the seats of questionable lavatories with toilet paper, but since seats are often missing as are all vestiges of toilet paper, one learns to hover, cantilevered, and never to leave home without a wodge of tissues.

The product advertised by Consumable Sales and Marketing in April 1990 would make a good alternative:

> If you're nervous of using public toilets, the recently launched Peace of Mind toilet seat wipes are the answer. Unlike toilet seat covers, the wipes actually disinfect the toilet seat from various germs which may be present due to the flushing action of the toilet. The product has been specially designed for public toilets and office buildings, marketed in a dispenser housing 200 wipes.

Airports world-wide are particular offenders in the sleaze stakes because of the human tides surging through them. Our airports are now under new management which bodes well, but as recently as September 1997, Robert Kirby was fulminating in the *Mail & Guardian*:

> I go to a booth. At Johannesburg International this can be a mistake. The booth I visited had only a third of its lavatory seat, sticking up like a vast sharpened plastic dagger. Someone must have torn off the rest of this seat in panic, for use as an emergency weapon against what looked like a moving wall of pugnacious e-coli bacteria glowing along the edges of the wall and floor...

On no account lift up any lavatory seat you find (there) because this will entail your having to touch it. And don't even think of sitting on it. If the seat is already up, don't on any account let your eyes drift to any inspection of what's taken up residence in all those yeastfields underneath it...

But most of all, don't look down into the bowl. I did and I have to tell you that there were skid-marks in there which were so old as to have become petrified like dinosaur footprints... At Jo'burg International you don't have to worry about being anally retentive; the lavatory bowls do it for you...

What makes these lavatories even more daunting is that they're all being used by people who have just eaten some airline food or are about to do so. In either case, they are shitting themselves.

Help is on the way, however – for women, at least. On 24 March this year, the *Daily Telegraph* reported on the very latest invention on the public convenience scene:

URINAL MAKES A STAND FOR WOMEN

A urinal for women was launched yesterday by a Dutch company, claiming it heralded the end of sitting on unhygienic public lavatories.

Women will stand with their backs to the 'Lady P' by Royal Sphinx Gustavberg NV, with legs slightly bent. Designer Marian Loth said she got the idea from a friend who visited the men's toilets when confronted by a long line for the ladies room.

Ms Loth said: 'Research showed that women hate using toilets in public places. They find them filthy and sometimes have a fear of sitting.'

Sphinx said it expects the Lady P, which was launched on Tuesday at a German trade fair, to be installed in public restrooms in airports, stadiums and restaurants throughout Europe.

USEFUL TIP FOR THE TRULY FASTIDIOUS:
A sociological study has found
that, in any row of toilets, far
more people use the ones in the
middle than those on the ends.

TIPS FOR TRAVELLERS

The first word to learn in a foreign language, before please and thank you, is 'toilet'. After that, learn the phrase for two beers.

Local tour operators and eco-activists are aware of the lack of decent public conveniences, and there have been two interesting developments in the Mother City. From *The Star*, 3 December 1989:

> City councillors in Cape Town have approved a plan to install condom-vending machines in public toilets. Not only 'regular' but 'extra-size' condoms will be on offer. The latter presumably for the benefit of visiting Transvaal holidaymakers. In the course of the council debate … it emerged that Cape Town still keeps to the quaint custom of referring to public toilets as 'chalets'. So it was quite imaginative for a councillor to suggest the city should make tourist capital of its 'impressive range of chalets'.

Cape Town anthropologist, Mercia Waring has had an even better idea. On 6 December 1997 Andrea Weiss of the

Weekend Argus wrote of her suggestion that a Loo Route should be planned to complement the Wine and Whale Routes and provide employment to the unskilled:

RELIEVING TOURISTS WITH A YEN FOR THE LOO

...Mercia says she has gained much insight into the state of the city's toilets through 'fieldwork' ranging from Simon's Town to central Cape Town and has found them to be lacking.

Her idea is to fill in the gaps by building more toilets and to supply tourists with an accompanying map detailing their whereabouts. In addition, Mercia envisages that each of the loos should be staffed by an attendant who will earn additional income by selling essential items...

In her quest she has spoken to the ANC and the DP, which in turn have referred the matter to the Cape Metropolitan Council.

Now what remains to be seen is whether her idea, for which she wishes to be paid, is about to be bogged down in bureaucracy. We may also add our pennyworth to this: given the current over-supply of parking 'attendants' showing us into parking spaces, perhaps we should consider diverting some to the job of ushering us into vacant toilet booths to park our bums?

Linda Stafford had already done pioneering fieldwork for *The Good Loo Guide* in *Signature,* February 1993 – which makes salutary reading for restaurateurs:

To my mind, the proprietor who neglects his loos risks ruining the entire impression he has been trying to create. He risks puncturing the *amour-propre* of his clientele; especially that of all-important female customers ... In the South African restaurant tradition, however, loos appear to come last...

The average local restaurant rest room – a misnomer, if ever there was – consists of a couple of loos, a basin and a mirror.

(Only the cruellest of restaurateurs omits the mirror). Its accessories are usually confined to an industrial-type canister of lurid pink liquid soap and either a grubby roller towel, rough paper napkins, or one of those terrifying blowers under which you are obliged to rub your hands for what can seem like hours...

In fact, you will often find that the better the restaurant, the worse its loo.

Among the restaurants Linda praised for their loos were Sausalito in Johannesburg, Benson's, Buitenverwachting and Tantina's in the Cape, Bloomers in Durban and White Mischief in Pietermaritzburg. All but one have closed or changed hands now, and dining out is the poorer.

London restaurants, ever in the forefront of fashionable dining, have discovered that unusual loos can be a positive drawcard. Quentin Letts wrote about the new trend in the *Daily Telegraph* on 14 March 1998:

If you are going to open a restaurant in the late Nineties, it seems that you need a gimmick for the loos... In the Gents at Oliver Peyton's new London restaurant, Mash, the urinal is a crazy-curved, proportion-warping reflective panel, as in a summer fairground's House of Mirrors. The Ladies, meanwhile, is equipped with small television sets that transmit live shots of what is going on in the Gents.

'The key to a good restaurant is getting everyone to interact,' says Peyton. 'I thought the cameras in the Ladies would give women a good laugh and I thought those mirrors were guaranteed to make every man come out with a smile on his face...'

Mash's lavs are ... a feature, just like the ones at Damien Hirst's new restaurant, Pharmacy, where the urinal is a mock-up of a chemist's cabinet, and Belgo Centraal, where the washbasins are such an odd shape that some have mistaken them for a pan...

Even the workers at C P Hart – loo-makers to The Ritz, Claridge's and the Savoy – say 'outrageous' is the way forward. 'Loos can be such boring places,' says a spokesman. 'I am all for moving towards a Philippe Starck-style, functional, minimalist design – perhaps with a bit of fun thrown in.'

Frankly, I would rather they didn't. Call me a prude, but when I go to the Gents I do not want to find guys shrieking with puerile laughter at the funny shapes they are making in the bendy mirror. Nor, particularly, do I want to be filmed by a camera which is linked to the Ladies.

Jenny notes: Belgo is a wonderful noisy restaurant in a cellar near Covent Garden where the waiters dress like monks and you sit at long tables ordering from a vast range of Belgian beers and a menu heavy on mussels and succulent sausages. The washbasins in the unisex lav are not only an odd shape – they appear to have no taps either. Confused new visitors need to be shown the foot-pedal that delivers a welcome gush of water.

DOING YOUR BUSINESS
IN LONDON ...

The *Sunday Star* of 6 June 1993 gave another useful tourist rundown – of the public conveniences in London's main railway stations voted the best by *Sunday Express* readers:

THE BEST OF LONDON PUBLIC LOOS

Make a note of them; they're easy to get to by underground and there is nothing worse than being desperate with nowhere to go.

King's Cross: Situated at Platform 8, this is the most homely of British Rail's offerings, despite being well used and covered in graffiti. There are fresh flowers in the wash area and framed pictures on the wall. Entry costs 10p and paper borders on the rough. There are baby-care facilities... A full-length mirror and a vending machine selling toothbrushes makes it a cut above the rest.

Charing Cross: Situated opposite Platform 1, these conveniences are an extremely clean, high-tech combination of deep purple mosaic and pink doors. Entry is 10p and the loo rolls are soft. The make-up areas are framed with individual shelves and there are also baby-care facilities.

Victoria: Situated at Platform 14, this is considered the Ritz of British Rail loos because of its 20p entry charge... Spacious, bright and modern, the decor comprises shades of grey and there is sunken lighting over the mirrors. There are baby-care facilities and soft paper, but it is a bit impersonal.

Euston: Located at Platform 3, these toilets are free, clean and functional, with soft loo paper and a toothbrush and travel-pack vending machine. There are mirrors for make-up but no baby-care facilities.

Marylebone: Entry is free to these toilets, which have an impressive oak door but little behind it. There are no baby-care facilities but there are free loo seat-covers.

NB: Hard-up South Africans should beware posh tourist traps. In early 1994 the luxury loos in Harrods were re-done in marble, fitted with phones, hairdryers, soft lighting, plush armchairs and uniformed attendants – and customers who don't possess Harrods cards were notified that it would cost them a pound to spend a penny.

Britain has (would you believe) a Golden Loo Award: a mahogany lavatory seat trimmed in gold braid for which there is fierce competition. It was won in 1984, according to a droll item in the June 13 *Fair Lady*, by the public lavatories at Covent Garden which sported scented soap, hand towels, drinking glasses, sweet music piped over a sophisticated stereo system, walls full of paintings and lots of artificial flowers.

Presiding over this congenial domain were two former stalwarts of the British Army: Les Harding, once a colonel's batman, and Reg Bedwell, who had been a staff sergeant with the Royal Artillery.

'What I say,' said Les, 'is that the public pays our wages, and the public deserves the best. When I got here eighteen months ago, you should have seen the place. So Reg and I had a discussion, didn't we, Reg?'

Reg nodded. He was not all that comprehensible as he had lost his teeth at Christmas...

'We chose the colours ourselves,' said Les. 'I said to Reg, what colours do you think, Reg, and Reg said to me, "I think we should have blue for the men and pink for the ladies..."' We buy the soap out of our own money. It's never nicked. And we play the music on records.'

At that moment Jim Reeves was singing *The Shifting, Whispering Sands*, but you can also hear Barry Manilow, Elvis Presley and Dean Martin. There are many tubs full of plastic flowers and china clowns perched between the cubicles... On Saturdays there are enormous queues outside. 'I don't know how they can wait so long,' says Reg.

... IN FRANCE ...

That same year, the inimitable Barry Ronge wrote a very funny piece in his November Table Talk column in *Fair Lady* titled THE CONTINENTAL DIVIDE, after a trip to France and the Far East. It reads in part:

> As we all know, no one is at greater risk from nature's calls than the tourist far from home. Strange food, unpredictable water and ruthless sightseeing routes pose problems of their own, but in addition to that, those comfortingly legible Ladies/Dames and Gents/Here signs are missing. They have been replaced by odd foreign phrases and, in the remoter East, by calligraphic symbols that are absolutely inscrutable...
>
> In France, for example, gentlemen are encouraged to use those circular *urinoirs* which dot the pavements of busy streets, in which a band of

curved metal serves the cause of modesty, leaving face and feet exposed to the world. Now perhaps I am an inhibited prig but there is no way I can relieve myself on a busy street with the world looking on, usually in the form of a busload of American tourists who stare in horror as if they have caught you – well, red-handed is perhaps not the apt expression, but at least red-faced.

One can only assume that the *Fair Lady* sub-editor substituted the word *urinoir* for the genuine article to spare the blushes of the gentle readers.

Visiting tourists have always giggled and pointed at *pissoirs*, though to us they're excellent examples (along with the bidet and *The Scandals of Clochemerle*) of French pragmatism in matters of personal and public hygiene. Alas, on a recent visit to Paris Jenny was saddened to find that the *pissoirs* on the Champs Elysées have been retired and the remaining circular screens converted to mere advertising hoardings or stalls selling newspapers, magazines and cigarettes. *Quelle horreur!*

It's a comfort to know that the puissant *pissoir* has migrated west. In 1991 foreign correspondent Ramsay Milne reported in *The Star* that New York city planners, keen to provide 400 new 'edifices of convenience', were unable to agree on a design that would fit on the narrow pavements yet keep out the homeless and drug addicts:

> A Monsieur J C Decaux, architect of Paris's finest wayside conveniences, was invited to display a model that might be regarded as the Cadillac of loos. He even presented a demonstration model to New York's Municipal Art Society.
>
> The society's members loved it. Not surprisingly, as M. Decaux's gleaming model among its many other attributes includes an elaborate self-cleaning system. This enables it automatically to

heat the bowl, dispense water and soap in judicious amounts, then retract the bowl into the wall, flush it and douse it with disinfectant.

M. Decaux's efforts paid off. On 2 July 1991 *The Star* reported:

NEW LOOS BOWL OVER NEW YORKERS

They're a little French, a little daring, and they do come in useful. More than that, New Yorkers have been bowled over by the city's new and very innovative public toilets that made their debut on the streets of Manhattan yesterday.

The circular, self-cleaning toilets, attractive to the eye with their decorative wrought-iron cupolas that make them look not unlike Victorian mail boxes, have been provided by a French company which won a multimillion dollar city contract.

Mayor David Dinkins helped open the kiosk-style loo behind the City Hall. But did he inaugurate it, asked a reporter? 'I didn't have the need,' explained the mayor, not amused.

To discourage loitering, the kiosk opens after 15 minutes.

Encouraging hygiene is just as important. A Sapa/AFP news item in the *Sunday Times* on 28 December 1997 read:

A Frenchman's mission to ensure better hygiene among restaurant staff has inspired him to invent a toilet which locks users inside unless they wash their hands. People are trapped in the toilet designed by Jacques Robaey until they put their hands under the sink taps for at least ten seconds.

The 57-year-old Dunkirk tiler set about

constructing a hygienic loo after seeing a television report a month ago, which revealed that a dish of peanuts put out by staff in a Paris bar contained traces of urine from various individuals. The toilet guarantees people wash before they leave through a system where the taps are set off by a photo-electric cell connected to an electric lock on the door. Robaey already has about 100 orders and financial backing for the toilet, which he is aiming at the restaurant and food industries.

... AND INTERNATIONALLY

Savvy municipalities in tourist areas understand the pulling power of attractive, well maintained public toilets. Reuter reported in April 1987:

> Shoppers in Vienna can again answer calls of nature in turn-of-the-century style. A 1905 lavatory complex, designed by Adolf Loos, re-opened last week in the Graben.
>
> Aquamarine metalwork in swirling Jugendstil – the Austrian form of art nouveau – surmounts the twin entrances. Staircases of purple and white tiles lead beneath posts labelled 'Damen' and 'Herren' to a temple of hygiene, shiny with mirrors, marble and brass fittings. In the 'Herren', swing doors with engraved glass separate a handsome range of urinals from a room with eight cubicles. Each has a wood-framed cistern, a ceramic bowl with mahogany seat and a washbasin with gold-plated tap.
>
> Access to a cubicle is granted for 80c by Paula Krug, a flame-haired former cabaret artiste who has travelled the world and is now in charge of the

most up-market water closets in her city...

Business has been brisk since the reopening and mayor Helmut Zilk has been among the patrons. But not all visitors descend the stairs out of necessity – many just pop down to admire the architecture and fittings.

The pulling power of a flame-haired cabaret artiste presiding over the 'Herren' must also be considerable.

Our favourite travel editor Carol Lazar had a good tip for tourists to less developed countries in the *Sunday Star* of 12 September 1993:

If you are visiting China, Turkey, India (great destinations but public toilets are dreadful), buy yourself a packet of thin gauze surgical masks, put a few drops of scent on them, then place one over your nose before you enter a smelly, unappetising lavatory.

Jenny's friend Wendy Thorburn would have appreciated this useful advice. During a walking holiday with her husband Eric in the Himalayas, they visited Kathmandu where:

There were no public toilets and in the morning there's a firing squad of bums doing their business on all the vacant lots. Being a shy Westerner and having run out of Imodium, I was desperate and went into a police station for help. All the policemen shook their heads, warning, 'No, no,' but pointed upwards. On the second floor it was the same: they shook their heads, 'No, no,' and pointed upwards. When I got out of the lift on the top floor, all the windows were open to disperse the smell from three piles of the stuff about a metre high... At least I was able to do my business alone.

China is currently bending over backwards to improve public hygiene in tourist areas. A June 1996 Sapa-AP news item reads:

> In the Beijing of the future, perhaps all toilets will be as charming as the Toto SW-710 with a ZGHD-1, which slides a clean plastic cover over the seat after use. A limousine of lavatories, it's a monument to China's efforts to take the strain out of going.
>
> After centuries of discomfort, Beijing is embarking on the huge task of bringing pleasant public conveniences to the capital of the world's most populated nation. Chinese officials call it a 'public toilet revolution', and to highlight its efforts, Beijing staged China's first ever lavatory exhibition yesterday in, of all venues, the Museum of the Chinese Revolution on Tiananmen Square.
>
> China needs new public toilets because its people, as they get richer, want to answer nature's call in hygienic surroundings, said the exhibition organiser, Lou Xiaoqi. And besides, he said, smelly toilets that foul many a Beijing street shock foreign tourists. Most are huts with a trench, over which people squat together in rows. In the summer, their stink makes them easy to find in the dark, and in winter they are cold and repellent.
>
> 'People can go a day without eating. But rare are the days when they go without a visit to the toilet. They are something we can't do without,' he said.

Improved toilet arrangements weren't only confined to Beijing. On 17 January 1996 Carol Lazar reported in her weekly column, *Lazarbeam*:

One way or another, this has been an extraordinary week...In Taichung, in the Republic of China, flushed with joy, eight happy young couples plighted their troth in a toilet.

Marriage is difficult enough anyway, but to begin a marriage in a toilet seems somewhat indelicate. Not so, said bride Chiu Chiu-kuei, who designed the R 3.6 million public park toilets. For the record, her groom Lee-Wong-tsong built them. 'This is our communal creation,' said proud bride and groom. 'Besides, it's the place that everyone visits most.'

She has a point. As has her husband. The loving couple were photographed taking their vows in front of the urinals tastefully decorated with floral arrangements. The urinals, that is.

Visitors to Singapore need to beware of transgressing local hygiene laws. A 1989 news item read:

Singapore's 'Loo patrol', on the look-out for public toilet users who fail to flush, have nabbed the first offenders under a new flushing law. Health inspectors have booked 17 people so far under the law which came into force on July 1 making it an offence not to flush after using a public toilet. The 17 were let off with a warning during a two-week grace period. Offenders are liable to a fine of about R 1 400 each time they forget to pull the chain.

By 1998 the laws had been tightened to include further transgressions:

SINGAPORE. - The country's leading daily newspaper had a stern message last week for public toilet users: don't stand on the seats, don't forget to flush, and watch your aim.

The story about sloppy rest-room habits came during the annual Clean Public Toilets Campaign. The *Straits Times* hammered home the point by identifying six types of uncivil lavatory behaviour, including standing on the seat, parents helping their infants urinate in wash basins – and poor aim.

'Some bad aimers are notoriously nonchalant about their lack of accuracy and think nothing about spraying urine all over the toilet floor. Give such people a wide berth,' warned the paper.

Singapore should take a tip from the Dutch. An item in the *Financial Mail's* Did You Hear? column on 20 February 1998 read:

A Dutch company has been hired to manage the international arrivals building at JFK airport in New York. Reason is its success in keeping urinals at Amsterdam's Schiphol airport spotless. It does so by having a fly engraved on each one's porcelain. Men can't resist aiming for it.

'Ja, we have reduced spillage by 80%,' says airport economist Aad Kieboom. 'It's a perfect example of process control,' adds his boss, Jan Jansen.

Jenny's most interesting foreign encounter was with Japanese public toilets: spotlessly clean ceramic channels that face away from the door with two foot-rests for the correct squatting position and a cowling in front to prevent unseemly splashes.

Barry Ronge was not so enchanted by a Bangkok convenience with:

> …an asymmetrical hole in the floor with what can only be described as footrests on either side. This is no comfort station, it is a fiendish test of the endurance of your thigh muscles.
>
> It was not meant for western dress so an alarming amount of disrobing has to be done, in a confined space, and at great speed. The situation is not eased by the certain knowledge that one wrong step could produce an accident which no traveller's insurance in the world is going to pay for.

Tim's *bête noir* in foreign parts has always been those two simple footprints on which you squat before a single hole. He knows this kind of toilet as 'starting blocks'.

BACK TO THE LOCAL SCENE

Pissoirs may be acceptable in Paris and New York, but resistance rules in Hillbrow. Peter Malherbe reported in the *Sunday Times* on 19 January 1992 that the open-air urinal in an alley in Banket Street – 'which has raised a stink among residents' – had to be given small brick walls on either side because people objected to the sight of men urinating in full view. However:

> Councillor Desiree Simpson this week dismissed the flare-up as a 'storm in a teacup'. She said she viewed the open-air urinal as an improvement on people urinating in alleys and on street corners all over the area, as they had done.
>
> 'Gone are the days when we can worry about modesty. With the influx of people into our area our major concern is health and public safety.'

Both privacy and modesty are at a premium in South African public toilets today – that is, if you can find one where the lavs actually have bolts on the doors, paper on the rolls and soap at the basins. It seems that only the garages on our national roads are keeping the flag of good hygiene flying. Spare a tip for the attendants' saucer next time you visit one. They deserve it.

HONOURABLE RETIREMENT

Public conveniences have their uses even after their reason for being has fallen away. Kippie's in the Market Theatre precinct in Johannesburg is a prime example of conversion. Barry Ronge wrote in the *Sunday Times Metro* on 1 March 1987:

> Who dismantles an old loo and then rebuilds it right in front of the grand entrance to a theatre? The Market Theatre, that's who, and if the scheme sounds a little daft, please remember that this is a very special loo that has undergone an important personality change.
>
> It is now Kippie's Bar, one of the highlights of the Market precinct development. The stylish old

Victorian loo, so full of character and atmosphere, used to be tucked away on wasteland next to the railway siding that runs behind the theatre.

Originally built to complement the Market's architecture, it seemed like the perfect structure in which to house the musician's jazz bar which hopefully will keep the Market precinct grooving till all hours of the night. The structure was carefully demolished and reconstructed without the familiar porcelain appliances, and with more suitable seating.

The man after whom it was named, Kippie Moeketsi, was a brilliant saxophone player. In a sad and touching tribute in the *Weekly Mail* later in March 1987, Gus Silber wrote:

In 1959 ... Kippie flew to London as a member of the King Kong African extravaganza, whose entourage also included trumpeter Hugh Masekela and songbirds Miriam Makeba and Letta Mbulu. Far away in spirit and place from the shebeens and dance halls of the Eastern Native Township outside Johannesburg, Kippie felt not so much overwhelmed as simply out of tune...

He came back home. It was the Sixties – a bad time for nostalgia. The rich, fruity tones of marabi began to give way to the fast, sharp tang of mbaqanga, and it was no longer fashionable to wear a white jacket and a black bowtie in a big jazz band, and it was no longer cool to blow the way Kippie blew.

But it was all he could do. He made some kind of living as a studio musician and a guest saxman ... but most of the time Kippie was a full-time professional victim of his own passions and frustrations. He drank; he smoked dope; he blew... 'I am a drug addict, an alcoholic, and a genius,' he would say...Kippie died, penniless and almost forgotten, in Baragwanath Hospital on April 17, 1983.

Perhaps the shade of the man who said, 'Jazz was the only thing I ever had to my name,' lingers on in the toilet-turned-bar that now bears it?

The proportions of public conveniences lend themselves to certain uses. A similar conversion to Kippie's was planned a year later in London:

> April 1990. - A Victorian public convenience beneath the pavement near London's historic Spitalfields Market is about to get a new lease of life – as a fashionable wine bar. The underground property is being offered for sale by auction with a guide price of between R130 000 and R172 000... The auctioneers suggest that the 15.24m by 4.8m chamber containing six toilet cubicles, 10 urinals, washroom, storeroom and attendant's office, would make an ideal restaurant, wine bar, shop or nightclub.

And then there was the couple who spotted a royal opportunity:

LONDON, 16 May 1987. - A young couple who spent R107 000 for a public toilet converted into a small house have doubled their money in eight months. The house, in Tunbridge Wells, Kent, has just been sold for R211 000.

SAFETY & SECURITY

Locks are an ongoing problem in public toilets: if they exist, they often jam, causing temporary panic. More usually

they've simply disappeared: James Clarke wrote in his *Star* Stoep Talk column of 24 June 1993:

In a rather exclusive restaurant (in Réunion) the lav had a glass door and lace curtain, no lock, and occupied the corner of a large room... No lock! The French know that the English go completely to pieces when they have to sit in a lav without a door key...

In France itself they have further refined the art of embarrassing tourists: they have women attendants sitting in the middle of the 'gents', usually knitting. You give them a few centimes as you leave...

Maureen Lipman, also a *Star* journalist, wrote on 21 October 1988:

A thrilling part of public toilets is the door which nearly locks.

No sooner have you let it all hang out than the door is pushed sharply inwards, causing you to shout in an hysterical soprano: 'Sorry! Someone in here! Won't be two shakes! Sorry!' You simultaneously shoot your foot up against the incoming door, crash your coccyx into the toilet rim, and pee on your other foot.

There are remedies for this dire situation, however. In *The Toilet Book*, Bill Oddie and Laura Beaumont suggest (with illustrations):

The old *leg up* is a widely used and very handy method of keeping an unlocked door closed;

providing the door is close enough and opens *inwards*. If, however, the door opens *outwards* you are in trouble...

But the problem really begins when you find that your extremities are in no way extreme enough to cope with the amount of space between you and the dreaded unlocked door. Now is the time to *look around*. Can you see a *toilet-brush*, a *broom*, a *mop*? A small *towel*? A small but fairly heavy bathroom *cabinet*? Are you wearing a *jacket*, a *cardigan*, a pair of *tights* or a *belt*?

Depending on which way the door opens you can use the above to do the following: ... Tie tights, belt, cardigan or jacket securely round door handle, making sure that you can hold the other end quite comfortably. Pull tightly until you are ready to leave the room... Use toilet brush, mop, broom to hold against door and push hard until the toilet operation is completed... Use small towel to cram under door and wedge it shut... Place small heavy cabinet in front of door...

And there are two more pages of useful instructions. It is a most entertaining book and well worth investing in if you can find a copy on a second-hand book sale – the ideal venue for the acquisition of toilet reading (see READING MATTER).

Public toilets seem to be the place of choice for drug addicts to shoot up. In an effort to discourage them by impeding co-ordination and making it more difficult to find veins, Amsterdam authorities installed blue lighting and in Switzerland the public toilets have strobe lights.

LADIES &
GENTS

A MATTER OF DELICACY

We forget, in an era where everything is supposed to hang out, that until very recently society was coy about the necessity of going to the toilet. Men excused themselves from polite company with gallant euphemisms. Women pretended household imperatives or brief indisposition in order to be able to retire gracefully from the room. Heaven knows how their internal plumbing worked at all when they were laced into tight corsets.

Even to be seen near a lavatory was social death in Victorian and Edwardian times. Agatha Christie wrote of her childhood:

> We were very delicate about lavatories in those days. It was unthinkable to be seen entering or leaving one except by an intimate member of the family; difficult in our house, since the lavatory was halfway up the stairs and in full view from the hall. The worst, of course, was to be inside and then hear voices below. Impossible to come out. One had to stay immured there until the coast was clear.

In his 1829 *The Emigrants' Guide*, William Cobbett gave a glimpse of the spiritual agonies English women had to go through on the voyage to the New World:

> As to the work of undressing and dressing, however, this is managed in a very decent manner... The greatest and most injurious inconvenience is, that the modesty of English women too frequently restrains them from relieving themselves by going to the usual place for the purpose, which place is,

and must be, upon the deck, and within the sight of all those who are upon the deck.

This reluctance, however amiable in itself (and very amiable it is), has often produced very disagreeable, not to say fatal consequences. That mode of relief has been pointed out by nature; it is indispensable to animal existence; retention to a certain extent is destructive; and the sufferings experienced on this account are very great. *French* women must be excellent sailors; but English women, or American women, must change their natures, before this can cease to be a subject of really serious importance.

Use every argument in your power to get over this difficulty with regard to your wife; lose no opportunity of overcoming her scruples; be very attentive to her in every circumstance and point attending this matter; and if she be in a state, from her sea-sickness (which is frequently the case) not to admit of removal from her bed, you must be prepared, not only with the utensil suitable to the case, but you yourself must perform the office of chamber-maid; and this, you will observe, must be the case in many instances, whether you be in the steerage or the cabin; for, as to her servant maid, if she have one, you are pretty lucky if you have not to perform the same office for her; for there is no woman on board able to go to her: a thousand to one they are all sick together; and as to any other man performing the office for her, where is such a man to be found?

In the pursuit of gentility the loo has provided the subject for immense linguistic creativity. People will do anything to avoid naming names. The Elizabethans called it 'the place of easement'. Now we have: 'the little girl's room'; the 'chamber of commerce'; the 'cloakroom'; the 'long-drop'; the 'Ladies & Gents'; the 'smallest room'; the Geordie 'netty' (from Italian 'gabinetti'?); the 'dunny' (originally from the British dialect 'dunnakin', but now Australian); the South African 'P.K.' (from 'picannin kia', meaning 'little house') etc.

The act of going there is also concealed with a dainty nicety. I'm going to: 'wash my hands'; 'see a man about a dog'; 'powder my nose'. When we were kids we'd say, 'I'm going to do "No. 1" or "No. 2"' (though we were never quite sure which was which!) During the Second World War a favourite was: 'I'm going to telephone Hitler'. The Australians are marginally less restrained – 'I'm going to splash the boots … point Percy at the porcelain … shake hands with the wife's best friend'.

In South Africa we have even gone through a transitional phase when there were still segregated toilets but the more open-minded could go to the 'International Toilets'.

We believe we should not sweep this thing under the carpet. We should be open and honest. We must, as they say in America, 'cut the crap' and ask of our hosts, 'Please take me to your euphemism.'

NAMES & DESIGNATIONS

Early names for the 'necessary house' have interesting derivations. That erudite humorist Frank Muir explained in *The Frank Muir Book*:

> 'Jakes' was the Elizabethan word for the lavatory. Actually a euphemism, as all names for the things are, including 'lavatory' which is the plumber's word for a wash-basin, 'toilet' which was a lady's dressing-table, and 'loo' which came from the

old Edinburgh custom of emptying the chamber-pot out of a tenement window with the cry of warning to pedestrians passing beneath – 'Guardy-loo!' 'Jakes' derives from 'Jack's place', a reference to the inventor of the appliance, Sir John Harington.

James Clarke, ever the canny observer of human behaviour, explained in his Stoep Talk column in *The Star* on 24 June 1993:

> The design of the French lav is their way of getting at the English-speaking world which, as everybody knows, is terribly self-conscious about lavatories. The English will not even say the word. They used to say 'water closet' ... and then WC. Then it got even coyer and became 'loo' – even so, they shuffle the feet in embarrassment when they mention it...
>
> The Americans are worse. They don't have a word for lavatory.
>
> They say 'bathroom'... I recall being told by Neil Armstrong that all three astronauts who went to the moon in 1969 came back seriously constipated because they were too inhibited to do anything about 'going to the bathroom'...
>
> The French call lavatories 'toilettes' which makes their lavs sound more refined than they are.

The elevated American circles in which James moves may not use their word for the lavatory aloud, but we commoners know it's 'john'.

The naming of conveniences can be controversial. Alan Robinson wrote in his *Star* column Robinson's World on 26 October 1990:

Ledbury, in Herefordshire, is one of those preferred places where genteel folk reside. But there is nothing genteel about the frightful row raging around the town's public conveniences.

The local council has just refurbished this essential amenity, but it seems workmen were intent on saving time and paint when they came to putting up their signs. They did a good job on the Ladies, and the Disabled won high praise from caring citizens.

But when the local squirearchy set eyes on the Gents, blood pressures rose and moustaches bristled. 'Appalling', 'slang', 'common', they howled. Neil Rabagliati, whose surname suggests forebears as English as macaroni, thundered: 'It (Gents) is a horrible word and quite inappropriate to Ledbury's style.' He insists only Gentlemen will do.

The council waded in clutching a copy of Fowler's *Modern English Usage*, which agreed that Gents is acceptable. Mr Rabagliati stormed out of his sixteenth century timbered house waving a copy of the *Concise Oxford Dictionary* in which the word does not appear at all.

THE GENTS

Quentin Letts had this to say about the ideal Gents in his *Daily Telegraph* article on 14 March 1998 about gimmicky restaurant lavatories:

> The Savoy, as so often, gets it right. Its lavatories are high-ceilinged, porcelain-lined sanctuaries. Silence reigns and an attendant, with little more

than a dry cough, will run you a basin of hot water and stand by with a warmed towel.

At Lord's, the lavatories at the Pavilion end were artfully designed with a long, horizontal window so that fans could watch the cricket while they stood at the urinal. The old clubs of Pall Mall and Mayfair also do this type of thing well. You may sometimes find that one tap is left dripping, but that is simply to assist older visitors whose waterworks may be playing up. And there is free shoe polish, the use of a clothes brush, and probably an old-fashioned, sit-down weighing machine.

The jovial camaraderie at the urinals in a Gents where most of the blokes know each other is highlighted by a Reuters dispatch from Canberra in August 1997:

Australian Deputy Prime Minister Tim Fischer ... says the flow of communication in the new parliament house has slowed to a trickle in the absence of the communal troughs which were a feature of the old parliament house, vacated in 1988. At the launch of a book of humorous political anecdotes yesterday, Fischer bemoaned the fact that humour has become more highbrow since it has been taken from the toilets to the tearoom.

'There is no doubt in my mind that the reason there is less humour in the parliament house is a design fault which would be greatly helped if we turned off all the plumbing in individual members' and senators' suites,' he said. This would aid the democratic process by re-establishing the rapport created by 'informal' contact, which is necessary for bipartisan decision-making, Fischer has insisted.

Former prime minister Gough Whitlam acknowledges that great communication took place in the loos of the old parliament house.

Robert Kirby couldn't disagree more. In his Loose Cannon column railing at airport toilets (see PUBLIC CONVENIENCES), he also takes aim at urinals:

> If there's anything worse than the smell of old cold urine ... it's the smell of new warm urine. Which is why I am of that select breed of males who believe that the act of micturition should be discreet. Something which takes place between you, your urethra and gravity. I simply don't like peeing up against a wall along with a set of complete strangers. This is nothing more than a mutated form of what dogs do when they piss all over the same parking meter. At least the dogs don't do it all at the same time.

THE DEMAND FOR POTTY PARITY

The biggest drawback of public loos is the difference in the speed of use. Because women need more privacy than men and take longer, their facilities are ill-equipped to handle crowds. The imbalance often results in the situation Jean Waite wrote about in *The Star* on 12 October 1983, when Sol's brainchild was the acme of weekend destinations:

> Sun City over a long weekend with a major star at the Superbowl is like a synthesised version of

Dante's Inferno. You queue to get into the car park, on to the bus, for the show, for the restaurants, for the bars, for the slot machines and, most desperately of all, for the toilets...

There is hardly a more ridiculous sight than a queue of women spilling from the open door of the women's toilet – with attendant husbands and boyfriends lurking impatiently a few metres away.

You might heave a sigh of distress at first sight of the foot-hopping line and decide to give it a miss. But if it doesn't get you first time round, you'll have to succumb in the end – it's a long drive home.

Toilet allocation had to change. Nine years later foreign correspondent Ramsay Milne was writing of another Superbowl in the *Weekend Argus* of 1 February 1992:

NEW YORK. - Last weekend's Superbowl marking the climax of the American football season may go down in history as the game that ushered in true equality for American women in one vital area: public toilets.

With the 80 000 crowd predominantly male, women spectators found themselves waiting in long lines outside the women's restrooms, with no queues outside the men's. One result is that fuming women, who say they have suffered from this kind of inequality long enough, are pressing their Congressmen to pass a Federal 'potty law' that will more fairly meet their needs.

The statistics are compelling. According to the American Society of Sanitary Engineers, women in restrooms take nearly twice as long as men (averaging about 80 seconds compared with men's 45 seconds), yet nearly all public conveniences have far more stand-up urinals than toilet seats for women. Ramsay Milne goes on:

> Six states have already passed 'potty parity' legislation. It is pending in 11 others. Under pressure from feminist organisations, most states have, in fact, gone beyond parity. In California, for every two toilets and/or urinals for men, there must be three toilets for women. In Illinois, there must be one women's stall for every 200 persons and one men's urinal and/or stall for every 425.
>
> Though 'potty parity' is giving comedians much grist for risqué jokes, it's no laughing matter. Clearly, 'potty parity' is a challenge no one is going to take sitting down.

Arnold Benjamin enlarged on the subject in his So it Goes… column in *The Star* in May 1992, when he reported that Florida had also passed a law requiring more toilets for women than men:

> The bill's sponsor, Senator Helen Gordon Davis, had a word for her achievement: 'I'm flushed with success.'
>
> Apropos, a quote from Britain's veteran Labour politician Tony Benn: 'Anyone who wants to see real division in society should go to the House of Lords, where the lavatories differentiate between peeresses and ladies.'
>
> And apropos again, a medical professor told a congress a while back that one in four Britons – presumably of either sex – fails to drink enough fluids, usually for fear of not finding a public toilet.

The South African judiciary has a long way to go when it comes to potty parity. In an article bemoaning the paucity of women judges in the *Sunday Times* on 8 August 1999, Carmel Rickard wrote:

WOMEN JUDGES DENIED A PROPER SEAT

...at least Parliament has sorted out the question of women's loos. Symbolically, perhaps, several of the old High Court buildings and the Appeal Court still have 'judges only' toilets, which are clearly intended for the use of men only. Women judges must use the facilities labelled 'secretaries only'.

There was a lot of misogynist growling in certain hallowed portals over potty parity. David Walker noted in his column Walker at Large in *The Star* on 20 July 1992:

Belatedly, I learn the real reason for London's Garrick Club refusal to accept female members. Before the vote was taken, one diehard warned of the mayhem which resulted when the Reform Club let women in. 'They wanted more loo space, they were militant and they made a bloody nuisance of themselves.'

Good thing the diehards hadn't heard of Frikkie Dreyer's invention or the growling would have grown to anguished howls. Caroline Hurry of *The Star* ran it to earth just before the Rand Show in March 1991:

Due to their biological persuasions, men have been known to relieve themselves from a discreet standpoint behind walls or against the nearest tree.

Women, on the other hand, have had to contend with the dubious sanitation of public toilets. However, the fairer sex can now make a stand, thanks to an innovative idea from Frikkie Dreyer of Barberton who has developed a disposable funnel to enable women to relieve themselves standing up.

'In the past, women had to resort to a number of ingenious devices to avoid coming into contact with a germ-laden lavatory seat,' says Mr Dreyer. 'Sitting on rolled-up newspapers or adopting an uncomfortable squatting position above the seat are just two of their options. My urinary aid for women comes with a full set of instructions, is easy to use and keeps them away from germs.' Mr Dreyer's disposable funnels are hygienically packed in a sealed plastic bag and also double up for use in the kitchen. The Eezy Wee costs R4.80 for a packet of 12 and will be available at the Rand Show.

THE PRINCESS AND THE PEE

Even princesses face the problem. Margaret de Paravicini in one of her Between the Lines columns in the *Saturday Star* in March 1989 quoted Princess Diana:

Said Her Highness with unaccustomed bluntness: 'The trouble with being a princess is it's so hard to have a pee.' The occasion was when she was forced to go up nine floors to a private loo at a function. The fairytale of the princess and the pee takes on new dimensions.

WHAT GOES ON INSIDE

The chaps hanging round patiently outside the Ladies are almost certainly making heavy jokes about what's keeping them so long. Judy Rumbold in the *Guardian Weekly* on 25 June 1993 gave some answers:

> For by far the most comprehensive view of Royal Ascot Ladies' Day, I recommend the ladies toilet on the third tier of the Grandstand. A group of women from Birmingham, got up like the wedding party from hell, are comparing hats ... (and) decide that Eileen's is the best. Why? What makes it any less hideous than all the others? Its redeeming feature lies in its capacious crown, which facilitates smuggling in of illicit booze. Eileen produces a brown medicine bottle that once contained antibiotics for her son's ear infection and proceeds to pour out six double gins.
>
> 'At the beginning of the day,' says Maud, one of a vast army of nylon-overalled attendants, 'they're ladies. At the end of the day, they're not.'
>
> Midday. Muddy stilettos are being washed in handbasins, and the distant sound of vomiting echoes across the tiled walls. Clearly, that scary netherworld between lady and not-lady is beginning to beckon its victims. Pimm's has been consumed, champagne quaffed, coarse chat-up lines exchanged.
>
> 'It's a hoot when they've had a few,' says Barbara, toilet attendant in the ladies nearest the main exit. 'When they accidentally lock themselves in the loo we have a giggle. The police come in and a great cheer goes up, then the ladies come out laughing with their drawers round their ankles!'

By 1.30, standards and decorum are dropping as fast as ineptly sewn hemlines. For help in the way of needles, headache tablets and tights, the ladies is a godsend. 'You'd be amazed at the things they ask for,' says Beryl, tossing her head towards her colleague. 'Last year, Pat sold her petticoat.'

Incidentally, California law also states that women may use the Gents if more than three people are queuing for the Ladies. Is nothing sacred? we hear horrified men asking. Well, no. To quote another chunk of Barry Ronge's column in *Fair Lady* about his travels:

> South Africa's rigid separation of everything, including the sexes, ill prepares the tourist for the fact that both sexes use the same facilities in France. The sight of the ladies in what has become, in other lands, the last impenetrable male bastion, covers you in confusion.
>
> You retreat to the pavement to hover desperately until you see another man go in and return, unscathed and unpursued by hosts of offended females; and so, suppressing your most fundamental training in favour of an even more fundamental need, you brazenly enter, flash a franc, and find blissful release.
>
> Not everyone can adjust. One of my unforgettable Paris memories is of an American woman of undeniable chic, but dire need, racing down the staircase, seeing me emerging, and bursting into tears because the relief she thought she had found had been so cruelly snatched away.

Cutesy-poo alternatives for Ladies and Gents are a staple of restaurants that are trying too hard. Adam and Eve, Madam and Adam, and Guys and Dolls are old favourites, as are the

Lads and Lasses in Scottish pubs for tourists and Bulls and Heifers in steak houses. The funniest pairing we've come across is Pointer and Setter.

Arthur Goldman, doyen of South African travel journalists and then editor of *Travel World*, spotted two new combinations in 1985:

> When in Florida, United States, recently, I paid a visit to the Bounty, MGM's movie recreation of Captain Bligh's ship for the Marlon Brando version of the historic mutiny. It is moored alongside the quayside of St Petersburg. The onshore loos had the following signs on the doors: Buoys and Gulls. Last time I was thus regaled was at the Chicago Pizza Pie Factory restaurant in London's West End... There the men's was dubbed the Elton John and the ladies' was titled Olivia Newton John.

BEWARE OF YOUR NEIGHBOUR

There are certain dangers to watch out for in the Ladies & Gents, as can be seen from the following two anecdotes:

> Wallace Reyburn recounts that while the famous music composer Eric Coates was relieving himself in a public lavatory, he heard the man next to him whistling his composition, *Knightsbridge March*. The man kept sounding the wrong note, however, and Coates leant over and tried to put him right. The man mistook his attentions, however, and it was only after an unfortunate scene that Coates was able to establish his innocence.

EXCUSES, EXCUSES

A peeping tom called Leon appeared before Magistrate P J Smith in Johannesburg in 1985, accused of 'impairing the dignity' of a young woman 'by peering over the dividing wall of a women's toilet in the Metropolitan Trust Building in Fox Street.'

He pleaded not guilty, saying that he had rushed into a women's toilet out of desperation as he had weak kidneys as a result of spinal injuries, felt stabbing pains and needed to relieve himself. He maintained that he couldn't have looked over the wall at the young woman because he was too weak to climb as he was recovering from paralysis caused by breaking his neck two years previously.

The magistrate found his evidence highly improbable and fined him R200 or two months' imprisonment.

A case of grievous toiletry harm?

ETIQUETTE

Consideration for others is essential if a toilet is shared by more than one person. The correct etiquette is summed up in two brief sentences... Don't hog the place. Leave it clean.

And there is an extra virtue required of gentlemen, as detailed in a *Sunday Times* dispatch from New York in June, 1987:

FROM A BED TO THE LOO, WHAT GENTS SHOULD DO

What makes a 30-year-old gentleman? According to experts on male manners, he should have made love at least 1 248 times by then with a minimum of 19 partners. He should also have spent a night in a jail, a brothel, a monastery and a youth hostel.

The attributes are among 99 so-called social graces listed by the American magazine, *Gentlemen's Quarterly*.

Their ideal 30-year-old isn't all macho – he should have had a one-night stand that he was ashamed of. And he has one truly redeeming feature: he knows how to clear a blocked lavatory.

Gentlemen! To arms! To plungers!

Staying with matters male, John O'Grady wrote a book called *Aussie Etiket – or Doing Things the Aussie Way* in which he details how a bloke should behave in a public bar, specially when it comes to standing his round (or 'shout') so that people won't think he's a 'bludger'. Then:

> After a few rounds you'll need the toilet, which is called the gents. And there is a recognised etiket for your behaviour in this place. You do not stand in front of the porcelain pews, or stainless steel trough, and ignore your neighbour. You are

expected to acknowledge his presence. Any one of the following three opening sentences will do:

'Gees, this is a relief.'

'A man's just a go-between, isn't he? In one end and out the other.'

'How do you stop these things?'

Such remarks will lead to a minute or two of pleasant, friendly conversation, and then you should return to your 'possie' at the bar.

It is not good form to visit the gents and then leave the pub without saying goodbye to your casual drinking companions.

Formal goodbyes, such as, 'Thank you very much, gentlemen, for the pleasure of your company,' are okay in saloon bars and lounges, but will earn you unfavourable comment in public bars. A simple, 'Well, that'll do me for now – be seein' ya,' is all that is required. Provided it's not your shout.

An ungentlemanly lapse in etiquette recorded in Jeremy Beadle's *Today's the Day!* caused a Washington scandal:

> January 1, 1877: *A piddling little incident* upset the wedding plans of rich sophisticate Gordon Bennett and his demure beloved, Caroline May. Bennett arrived, after imbibing a little too freely, to see his fiancée and her terribly proper Washington family. Stumbling into the sedate drawing room, he dimly perceived the fireplace, mistook it for a convenience and without so much as a by-your-leave, used it accordingly. In disgrace, the marriage was cancelled and he exiled himself to France – much to everyone's relief.

LIFE ON THE OCEAN WAVE

Brian Snaddon, who used to crew on yachts, has this useful advice to offer about deep sea etiquette:

'Going to the heads' on small sea-going yachts is a source of great anxiety to new crew members. The apparatus is usually housed in a mini closet up forward which, when inhabited in the correct attitude, barely allows one to close the door or even take strain.

Moreover the skipper when asked for instructions on how to work it seldom seems inclined to give precise details in reply, despite the fact that the exit vent is below the waterline and is therefore a hull-flooding hazard. He'll say something like, 'OK, open the upper gate valve and when it fills, go ahead. Then close the middle tap. When you're finished, open the middle tap and at the same time the one with the red paint splash on it. Be bloody careful to do it simultaneously or you'll sink us, OK?' He will then ignore you and go back to squinting up at the sails.

Small wonder that after contemplating the closet and its taps and tubes, one finally asks for a bucket in the sail locker rather than sink the ship with your pants down.

The best method at sea, I've found, is to poke your debagged derrière over the stern and proceed. This however calls for both timing and aplomb, since a following sea can make things entertaining and the close presence of fellow crew members makes for a certain amount of pertinent banter.

Not a situation for the hesitant sphincter!

> ## GOING TO THE HEAD
>
> In the eighteenth century the word 'commode' was used for a tall headdress made of lace or silk and supported on a wire frame. So if a woman was described as wearing a commode on her head it did not necessarily mean she was strangely attired.

THE QUESTION OF QUEUES

Queuing in a crowded Ladies is not for the faint-hearted, specially in winter when layers need to be unpeeled. Try and jump the queue to speak to a friend, and you'll be speared by death rays from narrowed eyes. Dare to move along the row of stalls to make more room for those behind and luck on an opening door ahead of the legitimate first in line, and you could be lynched when you get out.

The only consolation is being able to watch the parade of primpers and smile-checkers at the mirrors – and the gossip. Jenny (not Tim) has heard some classic skinder muttered in loo queues or called over the partitions. The buzzy anonymity of a crowded Ladies seems to invite private confidences.

Carol Lazar reckons she hit on a lulu in a *Star* Lazarbeam column on the use and abuse of cellphones on 7 July this year:

> The other evening I went to the cinema and during the interval, visited the cloakroom, which, like most women's restrooms, is pitifully inadequate. There was a long queue but it didn't matter, for from within a cubicle a voice carried.
>
> 'What do you mean you want to be a woman? We've been married for eight years and you're a man. No, of course I didn't notice you'd been wearing my clothes. What? You're at the airport en route to Cuba?'

Eighteen women standing in line listened, mesmerised by the unfolding drama within. Eventually the occupant emerged, her cellphone tucked in her hand.

'Let him go,' said one sympathetic sister. 'Get a new wardrobe,' said another, and the unhappy woman was comforted by the entire restroom of strangers.

Back in 1989 when Johannesburg audiences were still flocking to the Market Theatre, Margaret de Paravicini gave a heartfelt account of a half-time crush in her Between the Lines column in a March *Saturday Star*:

You should try the Market on a first night ... or Ster-Kinekor Sandton when Tom Cruise is starring ... (and you have) to face the female dilemma: whether 'tis nobler in the mind to suffer the second half with gritted teeth or to take arms among the serried ranks against a sea of troubles – and, by opposing, end them?

Ah, Shakespeare knew a thing or two when he wrote: 'Frailty, thy name is woman!'

Smiling to hide impatience, hoping you're not missing too much in the foyer, you take bets with yourself on how long the woman before you is going to be and if you'll get back in time for curtain-rise. There are moments of desperate calculation as you size up your opponents in this obstacle race, noting with gathering hope or despair the extent to which they are dressed. You can be sure that the woman staring at you so intently is not interested in ... the cost of your designer trouser suit – she's worrying about how fast you are with hooks and zips.

One could almost feel sorry for the male escorts kicking their heels outside if one were not so envious of the ease with which they manage their affairs.

Private queues are something else. Gerald Durrell wrote in *My Family & Other Animals* of his Aunt Hermione's habits:

'Really, Mother, you are impossible!' exclaimed Larry angrily. 'I was looking forward to a nice quiet summer's work, with just a few select friends, and now we're going to be invaded by that evil old camel, smelling of mothballs and singing hymns in the lavatory.'

'Really, dear, you do exaggerate. And I don't know why you have to bring lavatories into it – I've never heard her sing hymns anywhere.'

'She does nothing else but sing hymns ... "Lead Kindly Light", while everyone queues on the landing.'

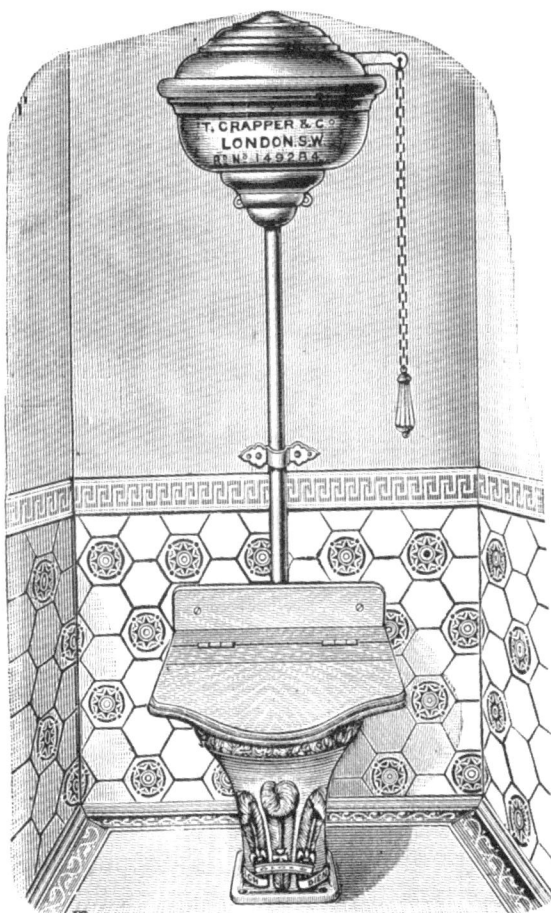

THE
THRONE

'The throne' is one of the world's great levellers, sat upon by everyone from commoners to kings and queens. Lucinda Lambton in *Temples of Convenience* makes a telling point about its lack of stature:

> The lavatory is an intimate friend to us all, and we should honour it as such. It is undeniable that a glorious throne with a welcoming wooden seat makes us laugh with pleasure. Why then do we minimise its importance, treating it as a mere receptacle, a necessary evil?

It wasn't so for grand folk in the old days. Alan Duggan told of a recently auctioned throne in the *Sunday Times* of September 1 1996:

Some people spend a lot of money on the smallest room in the house, furnishing it with everything from magazine racks to framed cartoons, and equipping it with the very best in sanitary ware.

Sometimes they take flights of whimsy, providing novelty toilet tissue ... or decorating the seat with flowers. In grander homes, they've even been known to install electrically heated seats with little sprays, blowers, and all manner of electronic aids. But, in the final analysis, a toilet is a toilet, right?

Not when it's a French-style eighteenth century satinwood and palissander serpentine commode, says British auctioneer Anthony Pratt. His Kent-based firm, Canterbury Auction Galleries, recently sold this fine example of the commode maker's art to an unnamed buyer for the staggering sum of R434 000.

The 1.14m wide item of furniture had a parquetry veneered top inlaid with sprays of floral marquetry. It was fitted with three long drawers, also richly decorated, and an apron with gilt brass mounts and sabots (wooden shoes).

Antique thrones are still available in specialist shops, at a price, and they're gorgeous: some with graceful moulded plinths in raised patterns and many decorated with patterns and flowers in a fetching indigo blue. Fine examples can be viewed in English stately homes operated by the National Trust and occasionally in turn-of-the-century South African mansions on show.

More to the point for anyone prepared to lay out a fortune for a fancy lav, there's been a return to decorative modern thrones, sometimes based on old designs. A cutting from the *Sunday Star* of September 13, 1992 shows the one bought by George Harrison:

> Collecting old loos must be a sign of the affluent class in Britain. Prince Charles admitted to a collection of antique lavatories this year, and now ex-Beatle George Harrison has bought for himself a fancy oak loo with faience trim and inscriptions, and a gold pull chain to flush it.
>
> Harrison purchased the loo from a Paris boutique called La Fontaine Amelie which specialises in fine reproductions of period water closets. The WC is tall and comfortable and is designed for more than bodily needs after a hard day's night. One can relax, read and compose in comfort on such an item in the bathroom, which may be a sign of our times that the only private place a man can call his own is the family bath and water closet.
>
> Harrison's new loo features a raucous French poem inscribed on faience on the tall back, and

will surely serve as a French lesson for English-speaking chaps at the ex-Beatle's house who have more time than lady friends to read the thing as they stand to relieve themselves in awesome style.

(If you're keen to be a sitting monarch in your own home, the same throne appeared a few years ago in a Sanitary City advertisement as 'The Maurice Herbeau Dagobert throne toilet'.)

An American jeweller with a penchant for pricey gimmicks has already created the ultimate toilet seat for contemporary grand folk, as *The Star Weekend* reported on 26 April 1986. Two colour photographs of a magnificent golden seat with a matching lid bearing a jewel-encrusted crown motif are captioned:

A THRONE FIT FOR A KING

This golden 'throne' is said to be the most expensive toilet seat in the world. Made of 24 carat gold plate and studded with 353 precious gems – including rubies, diamonds and sapphires – the seat is priced at $250 000. San Francisco jeweller Sydney Mobell's magnificent seat (he has created other such luxuries like solid gold mousetraps) is considered to be the ultimate gift for someone who enjoys sitting quietly in the lap of luxury.

Naturally, the trend caught on in Hollywood. On 19 January 1992 the *Sunday Times* reported:

STARS GO POTTY OVER LOOS

Luxury loos are the new seats of power in Hollywood and stars are splashing out to have the best. BMWs and tables at top restaurants are out and super bathrooms are in, says movie mag *Première*.

Producer Steve Tisch takes the magazine's best loo award – with a £150 000 'fantasy' toilet made of slate, glass and marble with a shower for four – and a waterproof phone.

Steven Spielberg has a jacuzzi and TV in his prize toilet... Producer Rob Cohen has a walk-in fridge stocked with soft drinks and crisps for guests – but refuses to install a phone saying top stars 'don't want to be reached on the john.'

Certainly, famous sitters add cachet to even the plainest pan – and the media love a good loo story. In 1985 *The Star* carried two photographs, months apart, featuring a London woman and her unusual acquisition. The first, in March, showed her in a dignified pose behind an ordinary white toilet truncated at the top of the S-bend. It was captioned:

> Mrs Edome Broughton-Adderley, a collector of unusual and royal memorabilia, in the drawing room of her elegant Chelsea home with her latest acquisition – Mrs Margaret Thatcher's loo, which had been dumped by the builder during renovations to the Prime Minister's former home in London's Flood Street. Although, as Mrs Broughton-Adderley admits, it is not in the same historical league as some of her other purchases, such as Queen Victoria's knickers, 'Who knows what Cabinet reshuffles might have been planned while she was contemplating there?'

In November *The Star* ran another photograph of her, this time kneeling behind the toilet which now had a plaque inside the raised lid and a bunch of grapes dangling from the seat. The caption explained the circumstances, then went on to say:

> Mrs Edome Broughton-Adderley now uses it as a very posh plant pot or 'jardinière' as she likes to call it. The notice says that Mrs Thatcher sat there from 1967-1979 … surely not – it couldn't have taken her 12 years to decide on her suggestions for the Speech from the Throne. It is not difficult to imagine her sitting there in her times of triumph, flushed with success, or when facing adversity, starting a chain reaction which would culminate in a Cabinet reshuffle. Anyway, Mrs Broughton-Adderley, it isn't everyone who can boast of having a former seat of government in her home.

Toilet design is moving on, you will be glad to know. In May 1999 *The Star* ran a photograph showing a man smiling proudly next to a sturdy white toilet with its ceramic rim broadened to hold two bright red footprints, captioned:

> Malaysian inventor Yap Wang Han presents the 'Squasit toilet bowl to squat and sit on' at the International Exhibition of Inventions in Geneva last week.

Dual purpose seems to be the phrase of choice in architecture today.

AS FOR THE PLUMBING ...

Erma Bombeck made people laugh for decades by sending up suburban housewives and their problems. In *The Grass is Always Greener Over the Septic Tank* there is a piece called 'Finding the Builder Who Built the House (1945 - 1954)' which will strike a chord with every first-time homeowner. His name was Edward C Phlegg and he had disappeared along with all his subcontractors...

'I don't want to panic you,' said my husband, 'but I think we're stuck with our own repairs.'

'Why should I panic? Just because when our water pipes sweat you prescribed an anti-perspirant? ... Just because you were too embarrassed to ask for a male or a female plug at the hardware store? ... Just because we have the only toilet in the block reseated with Play Doh...'

'Look,' he said, 'did you marry for love or did you marry to have your toilet fixed?'

When I didn't answer he said, 'I'll get my toolbox and we can talk about what has to be done...'

The search for Edward C Phlegg continued for nine years ... then one day we ... saw that he had died. His funeral was one of the biggest the city had ever known. There wasn't a dry eye in the church. We were saying goodbye to the only man ... who alone knew the secret ingredients of our patios that bubbled when the sun hit them. Who would take with him his reasons for slanting the roof toward the centre of the house and burying the septic tank under the living room floor.

From a nameless book that disappeared in Jenny's first publisher's move comes this useful tip for women (luckily she had photocopied the page):

Emergencies: *The blocked lavatory*: This can cause blind panic and appalling scenes. Ludicrous objects have obviously been thrust down your pan. Newspaper and toupés, hand luggage and God knows what. Keep a four-inch plunger on a three-foot rod (this costs about £1.25, and saves hours unbending wire coat-hangers and fishing unsuccessfully in unsavoury waters). Put the emphasis on the 'plunge up' rather than the 'plunge down'.

If the plunger fails, viz. you've given your all and so has it, and when you flush triumphantly it still wells upwards alarmingly (there's no stopping it), don't do-it-yourself. You need men down your man-hole. Get the pros in.

There is only one thing worse than a blocked loo and that's a loo that leaks. The steady trickle of water accompanied by the relentless hissing of the cistern's inlet valve is enough to drive anyone to insanity. A Durban man called Terry McAllen published a basic D.I.Y. handbook for women in 1980 called *"Leaky Loo's" And other views...* which starred a svelte redhead called Handy Hannah in jeans and bandanna doing household repairs. Here are two useful tips from it:

Most people's remedy for a leaky Loo is to give it a resounding kick or thump in a designated spot. The lucky ones are rewarded with a gurgle and a clunk followed by blessed silence... Nine times out of ten the problem can be traced to the ball valve ...

relatively inexpensive and not difficult to fit, but before going to that extreme try out the following:

1. Check to see that the ball is not too high. This can be done by lifting the valve till it shuts off the water supply, and then see if the water reaches the overflow. If this is the case you can generally solve it by bending the arm to set the ball lower.

2. Waggle the ball up and down a few times. It may be just a bit of muck jamming the valve.

The tenth problem is likely to be a perished rubber washer. Speaking as the Ms Nimble Fingers who recently replaced not one, but two rubber washers in leaking cisterns after two grown-ups had spent half an hour on each occasion working out how to unhitch the ball valve mechanism and then replace it, Jenny would send for the plumber if the resounding kick fails. If the leak is from the cistern outlet pipe, call him *tout de suite*.

NOT FLUSHING LIGHTLY

Waterborne sanitation may be one of humankind's greatest blessings but sadly it does not extend to the vast majority who lack piped water. Those who live in areas where water is scarce also need to be circumspect with their flushing, either resorting to bricks in the cistern or following the advice of the Scots relative who warned our friend Liz: 'When it's no' important, don't pull the chain.'

South African droughts have concentrated our sanitary engineers' minds on the relative merits and capacities of cisterns. As far back as 23 September 1983, Stephen McQuillan reported in *The Star*:

TOILET VANDALS MAY HAVE MET THEIR WATER-LOO

Benoni industrial designer Mr Brian Harmer hopes to be flushed with success next month when he enters his water-efficient WC for an inventiveness award. The water flowpath – the critical part of the invention – almost drove Mr Harmer round the bend as he repeatedly redesigned the channelling...

Three years of intensive design and a succession of prototypes were needed before Mr Harmer's new WC was ready to make a splash in the marketplace... The designer now claims 'most of the manufacturers in this country' are bowled over with the idea.

Drought and vandalism were two main factors prompting Mr Harmer to invent a vandal-proof closet that uses only 4½ litres a flush. The seat of the problem was to make a WC effective against attempted misuse by employing several tested metals. Mr Harmer eventually surfaced with a design that would fit together with a minimum of labour and use standard plumbing constructions.

'The WC had to take into account a highly efficient flushing action – making sure the entire contents were removed – and construction sturdy enough to defeat vandalism,' he said. 'Most efficient cisterns deliver between nine and eleven litres, so I have reduced that by at least half.'

And with South Africa's water shortage, he said, the timing of the design was more than a convenience.

Within a few years the Los Angeles city council was also tackling the problem. The following short piece appeared in the August 1 1988 *Time* magazine, with matching photograph of a technician quizzing a ceramic bowl in the testing lab:

ROYAL FLUSH FOR A FULL HOUSE

LOS ANGELES. - During this summer's severe drought, Los Angeles has adopted a typically high-tech approach to water use. The city council has passed an ordinance requiring that all new buildings be outfitted with ultra-low-flush toilets that use only 1.5 gal. of water, far less than the old 3.5 gal. variety. Problem is that the city needs 100 000 of these newfangled devices a month, far more than manufacturers are turning out.

Further complicating matters is the failure of the city's testing lab to quickly approve the three low-flush models available. To win city certification, a toilet must be able to flush eight handfuls of tissue. One model flunked when it flushed only seven.

You'll be glad to know that ...

SAPA reported in October 1991: United States city officials are recycling water-guzzling toilets into highway paving material. The toilets are stripped of their metal, crushed into fine porcelain and mixed into road aggregate.

A CHEAPER WAY TO NOBBLE A THIRSTY CISTERN

A new, more user-friendly option than the traditional brick was reported by Melanie-Ann Ferris in *The Star* on August 23 1999:

GET A HIPPO TO HELP YOU SAVE WATER

How do you save water? Easy – put a hippo in your toilet. No, not the large mammal but an innovative device which could save South Africa millions of litres of water per day.

The Hippo is a specifically designed plastic bag which is placed in toilet cisterns and can reduce water usage by up to 3.5 litres per flush, and water consumption by up to 10%. Six million Hippos are already in use in the UK and the company is hoping to sell five million in South Africa, saving about 100 million litres of water per day.

Furthermore, the Hippo Water Saver company has dreamed up a clever way to flog their wallowing wares by encouraging an early taste for capitalism: it is approaching schools. Each pupil or teacher will receive 10 Hippos to be sold at a cost of R10 each, of which the school will keep R5.

Right, class! Take out your Entrepreneurial Skills textbooks. Hands up all those who have sold their hippos.

FLUSHING USELESS, ACTUALLY

Low-flush toilets have distinct drawbacks, according to a classic example of lavatory reportage by Francis Temman of Washington in *The Star* on 5 August 1999, just as we were going to press. It certainly lifts the lid on a new line in black market trade:

AMERICANS GOING LOO-PY OVER SMALL TOILETS THAT OFTEN AS NOT FAIL TO FLUSH

A rising tide of consumer frustration over five-year-old government rules requiring low-flush toilets ... has spread across the entire nation and washed up in Congress.

Under federal law, all toilets made, sold or installed in the US as of 1994 must have a tank no larger than 5.7 litres – half the previous size. The aim was to conserve water – a laudable goal in a country where water demand has been dangerously outstripping supply for years. But the result has been a public outcry over private loos.

Representative Joe Knollenberg has written a bill to ease federal toilet restrictions. He says angry constituents have been flooding his office with complaints over the low-flow johns.

'My office has received thousands of phone calls, letters and e-mails from disgruntled customers who are angry that their new toilets repeatedly clog, require multiple flushing and do not save water,' he told a congressional committee recently. 'The message is clear. Get the federal government out of our bathrooms.'

But so far, his bill has been stuck in the congressional digestive tract – delayed in part by the Monica Lewinsky/Bill Clinton scandal...

Consumer advice columns in the nation's newspapers have been overflowing with letters from outraged flushers dumping their anger all over the new high-tech latrines...

Regulations set by the Texas Natural Resources Commission are even stiffer than federal laws. The result has been a thriving black market in the Lone Star State in used older models and therefore much larger commodes. Deanna Jones, who owns a second-hand shop in Ada, Oklahoma, travels to Dallas at least once a week to stock up on used thrones at regular auction sales there. 'People don't want these new, ridiculous little toilets.'

There are alternatives – high-tech, 'ultra-low-flush' toilets, equipped with electronic, pressurised water jets that transform a little trickle of water into a powerful torrent. But their price is prohibitive – up to $1 000, and they save only slightly more water.

'Ultra-low-flush toilets is a misnomer,' says Keith Riley, president of the Plumbing, Heating and Cooling Contractors Association of Southern California. 'You have to hold the handle down longer if you have solid versus light waste,' he says, choosing his words carefully.

One perverse effect of the US law has been to create a black market trade across the well-watered Canadian border, where laws are much looser. 'In Canada, it is legal for individual American citizens to purchase the 16 litres per flush toilets for installation (though) not for resale,' says Riley.

Many small traders do a tidy business in Canadian water closets – to the frustration of US

Customs agents and regulators. Toilets can swallow up 45% of the typical home's water consumption, or 50 000 litres of water each year to flush away 600 litres of waste.

With our increasing water problem in Southern Africa, specially in the drought years, we can expect similar laws in due course governing the size and efficiency of new toilet cisterns.

Interested second-hand dealers should start stockpiling now.

In Holland, the Frisians perform the same function as Van der Merwe in South Africa. Their heads are supposedly flat at the back. The reason for this, say the Dutch, is that every time they take a drink of water, the lavatory pan keeps hitting them on the back of the head.

BOGROLLS

HISTORICAL PRACTICE

The Romans used sponges; rural Americans have been known to employ corn cobs; desert people use sand (which makes them a hardy and nomadic lot); and books were used so often in the eighteenth century that a special word (bumfodder) was created for them – giving rise to the modern word bumf.

> It is not certain to whom credit can rightly be assigned for the invention of the ingenious perforated toilet roll, although the date of the advent is known. In 1880 the British Patent Perforated Paper Company came into being and at around the same time two Philadelphia brothers called Scott, a name to become famous in the tissue world, turned from the marketing of wrapping paper to meeting the demand for this newfangled style of toilet paper.
>
> (Wallace Reyburn: *Flushed With Pride*)

Jenny's Dad loved puns and limericks. She remembers him in his final year, felled by a heart attack and then a stroke, lying in his hospital bed chuckling like a schoolboy at the naughty verses being tossed back and forth between the trout-fishing friends who had come to cheer him up. He started fishing in the Berg when he was five and must have fished every promising stretch of water in Natal until he died at 79. Among many gems of the genre, he taught his kids when they were quite small:

In the days of yore before the war
When paper weren't invented,
You wiped your arse
upon the grass
And went away contented.

Bogrolls are still rare in poor countries where dry grass is available and non-tourist India where washing with the left hand is the traditional practice (and westerners who do it with paper are considered unclean).

Before the luxury of baby-soft toilet tissue, long-drops sported torn squares of newspaper or piles of old telephone directories and magazines, while townies used horrid little shiny squares that had to be vigorously rubbed between the hands to attain even minimal absorption. As John Cundill wrote in *When Last did you Pull the Chain?* (see NOSTALGIA):

> Remember when the only paper provided was that hard, slippery, translucent stuff that came in rolls or boxes? What took Western civilisation so long to come up with such a simple, soft solution?
>
> My children, who have never given it a thought, will never know how the modern toilet roll arrived on the scene as one of mankind's greatest blessings.

Tim remembers these Jeyes squares very well from his days at university in the Eastern Cape. They were of exactly the same texture as grease-proof paper and as effective (see his poem at the end of this chapter).

> In the old Rhodesia during UDI and the guerrilla war, locally-made toilet paper was known as 'John Wayne loo paper'. It was rough, tough, and took no crap.

Toilet paper is also a favourite subject of columnists. Carol Lazar wrote a classic piece titled *A SLAVE TO TOILET ROLLS FOR 25 YEARS* in *The Star* of April 4 1993 which began with a familiar plaint:

> Why is it that my family is unable to replace empty toilet rolls? And I am not the only sufferer in South

Africa. As you read this, hundreds of other mothers are tearing their hair in desperation because they are surrounded by empty toilet-roll holders.

Can it be that, contrary to belief, the assembling of a toilet roll is an intricate, intellectually demanding skill that, like childbirth, only a mother is capable of?

The response from the public was overwhelming. The following week Carol was (so to say) on a roll:

> I had no idea that my last column would cause such an uproar... The phone has not stopped ringing... Emmarentia van Greunen of Mondeor was succinct: 'Life's too short to thread a toilet roll holder.' For Dolly Thlabana, it was a political issue. 'I have been working in Houghton for 27 years, and always, I put in new toilet paper. My madam doesn't even know where the toilet paper is kept. I am the hand that has wiped this family's bottoms. When I read your column, I thought, Enough!'

Two years later in June 1995, Carol unveiled another dilemma in her *Star* column Lazarbeam:

Have you ever tried to open a new roll successfully? ... There is no way that the first end piece parts from the rest. You have to gouge your nails into the roll and tear off a wad which means that you're left with bits of torn, loose paper that are most unsatisfactory. I have actually studied the wad and do you know that on each one, there is usually a minimum of eight pieces of toilet paper?

What a waste. If you consider how many trees are needed to produce toilet paper, you will realise that it would be in the national interest to have toilet paper rolls that opened with ease.

BETWEEN THE SHEETS

Bogrolls are not the homely, inexpensive product they may seem; they have their standards and frequently generate price wars. A report by *The Star*'s Nikki Whitfield in May 1996 opened with the classic sentence:

> Shoppers watch out – you might think you're spending less of a penny on toilet paper, but you could be getting a bum deal...
>
> Problems were being encountered by shoppers confused by the price differences between one- and two-ply rolls, single and multipacks, and dastardly imposters in plain wrappers with no reference to ply or sheet count. The South African Bureau of Standards' controller of regional offices of trade metrology was firm about requirements:
>
> The number of sheets on each roll of toilet paper is stipulated by government regulation. And the law is clear: two-ply toilet paper must contain 350 sheets; one-ply must hold 500.

Back in 1984, there'd been a furore in Harare over bogrolls. The *Sunday Star* reported that a Zimbabwean toilet-roll maker was claiming that customers were being ripped off by inferior rolls that varied between 180 and 270 sheets; a bigger core had been used that made them look thicker than they really were. Nonsense, replied the opposition. The sheet-count method is also open to abuse through the use of inferior, thinner paper and reducing the size of the sheets.

Price wars began to rage soon afterwards and still erupt from time to time. In 1987 the *Weekend Argus* reported:

The humble toilet roll has become the soft focus of South Africa's hottest price war. With nine manufacturers vying for the bottom line, rolls are flooding the market and are sold at a loss.

The manufacturers handled the situation in the classic way: bamboozle the consumer. The sales director of a large tissue company admitted, 'Frankly, we are not making any money on single rolls which sell for as little as 29c. So we are subsidising the sales of singles from the profits on multipacks.' A survey showed that buyers of a supermarket 12-roll pack ended up paying more than R2 for the plastic bag – equal to another seven single rolls.

Where does this leave the consumer? Comparative long division in the supermarket is an option, but the main problem is that shortcomings only become apparent when the paper runs out – and who's counting?

THE COMMODITY ROLE

Inspired by the continuing bear market in 1996, James Clarke suggested a new angle in his Stoep Talk column in *The Star* – bogrolls as commodity:

Invest in double-ply treasure: a roll in the roof is worth more than a bar in the bank.

The toilet roll has shown an increased value even in the worst recession. Just look how it performed in the early 1980s – while gold came down from $800 an ounce to a quarter of that, the toilet roll doubled its price...

If you had invested R10 000 in gold at that time you would, before the 1980s were out, have been worth R2 500. If you had put that R10 000 in toilet paper you would have been worth R20 000. And if you had held on to the toilet rolls till today your stock would be worth R250 000...

Toilet rolls are light and wonderfully transportable and you won't get mugged if you carry them around. You can carry a dozen over your shoulder by pushing a broomstick through them... It is a form of wealth one can flaunt.

But, I hear people asking, how do you store them? Simple. You store them in the roof of your house where, of course, they become a wonderful form of insulation against the cold, affording a considerable saving in electricity.

Most important is that there are things you can do with toilet paper far more comfortably than you can do with gold bars.

Tim has long harboured a similar idea, but with Scottish kippers rather than toilet rolls. He has observed that they have out-performed other commodities and currencies. He suggests purchasing as many packets as possible, placing them in a safety-deposit box in the bank, and simply letting the investment mature. Bank robbers will be highly unlikely to choose that box, too.

James Clarke may be right about not getting mugged, but theft of bog paper is rampant. On 10 November 1991 Janet Wilhelm wrote in her *Sunday Times* column:

Do you know what priority invention the country needs? ...As you read this there are people hunched over drawing boards putting in overtime trying to come up with the perfect theft-proof toilet roll dispenser.

It's astonishing the lengths people will go to steal the most trivial things. So designers are having to pit their talents against a group of latter-day suburban rustlers – women willing to strip naked in a public loo and wind toilet paper around parts of their body. All for the dubious pleasure of taking home a free roll. And they earned their odd name because they rustle as they shuffle along trying to get to the exit.

I owe this illuminating nugget of information about the pilfering ways of women to the security manager of a large shopping mall. And he adds that rustling has no racial barriers – everyone does it.

Killarney Mall had already addressed the problem in a fiendish manner. The *Financial Mail* reported on 13 March 1987 that:

> An FM staffer has learnt the hard way that loo paper facilities in the (male) six-seater in Anglo's Killarney Mall have been all but wiped out. The standard roll in each cubicle has been replaced by two dispensers in the wash-up. Only a few yards difference, agreed, but still a long way to travel bent double with your pants down.

Things have deteriorated even further in some public buildings. A short item in the *Sandton Chronicle* of 17 June 1998 noted:

> If you go down to the Sandton Traffic Department today, you're sure of a big surprise! For if you should happen to need the public loo, make sure you take not only your own toilet paper with you, but also a loo seat. The Greater Johannesburg Metro Council

does not, apparently, deem it necessary to replace stolen toilet seats, provide loo paper – or even light bulbs, if you need to see to pee – so be warned!

WORLD ROUND-UP

France is a country where the money falls apart and you can't tear the toilet paper.

– Billy Wilder

Diplomats are adept at obtaining what they need to remain staunch at their appointed posts. In September 1984 when war was still raging in Mozambique, Clyde Johnson of *The Star*'s Lowveld Bureau reported:

> The 180km road stretch between Maputo and Nelspruit could be named the 'diplomatic paper run'. For it is along this road that foreign diplomats in the Mozambique capital travel to South Africa to get toilet rolls and other essential goods often missing from Maputo shops.
>
> Diplomats, repelled by the thought of having to use back copies of party newspapers instead of velvety tissues, long for the day they see the neon lights of Nelspruit's supermarkets looming up.

In distant Peking, November 1986 heralded a panic in the privy. The *China Daily* reported a massive run on toilet paper by consumers worried about rumours of stocks running out and impending price rises. Local entrepreneurs were jumping on the bandwagon too:

Toilet tissue prices in the Chinese capital have been lower than surrounding areas ... a roll costs only 15 fen (about 9c). When people living outside Peking found that the lower price could help them make money, they started buying up large amounts. Many vegetable farmers came into the city with carts full of vegetables and went out with carts full of toilet paper.

Further east, Japanese capitalists tightened their belts in November 1993 by dishing out dirt instead of dividends. The *Financial Times* reported:

TOKYO. - Fund managers investing in Japanese stocks may find themselves with a pile of manure and toilet paper. Forced to cut dividends as earnings are hit by the country's prolonged economic slowdown, companies are starting to compensate shareholders with produce instead...

Comson, a farming machinery maker listed on the Osaka stock exchange, says that instead of dividends it sent its 1 900 shareholders bags of fertiliser made from manure and sludge, while Nippon Paper gave 24 rolls of toilet paper to each shareholder. The move also helps companies reduce inventories.

Japanese scientists had already made their contribution to the management of sludge. An April 1991 news snippet reads:

PONGLESS PAPER FROM SEWAGE

HONG KONG. - Japanese scientists can now make paper out of sewage. Senji Kaneko, head of the Yokohama Sewage Department's technology-development division, says the paper is made by heating dehydrated sewage, then spinning it before mixing it with wood pulp in a seven to three ratio. There is no smell, he says.

Definitely a case of what goes around, comes around.

Even more serendipitous recycling took place in Kiev in November 1994:

> Some of Ukraine's increasingly worthless interim karbovanets currency has found itself being recycled as toilet paper. Each month, a paper mill in the city of Dnipropetrovsk is turning about 35 tons of old banknotes into items such as toilet rolls and wrapping paper.
>
> 'We get top quality paper from the bank notes. Only the colour – blue, pink or green – gives away what it once was,' said Vladimir Vereshchak, director of the paper mill.
>
> **(Report by *Reuter*)**

NEW YORK. - An American company claims to have wiped out the opposition in one of the world's least-heralded but most important contests. Wisconsin Tissue Mills Inc now holds the record for producing toilet paper at the rate of about 1 850 metres a minute, 24 hours a day... The West Germans boast they have hit speeds of almost 1 900 metres a minute but have failed to hold the record because their rate was achieved in bursts.

Andrew Walker in the *Sunday Star*, 13 January 1985

A cheeky effort to improve the product by Kimberley-Clark went awry recently. In April 1997 *The Times* reported:

> One of Britain's foremost scientists is suing the makers of a leading brand of toilet paper. Sir Roger Penrose claims that (manufacturers) Kimberly-Clark used the

mathematical pattern he designed 20 years ago to produce a lavatory paper that is super-absorbent and gentle on the skin. He is furious that the Penrose Pattern was used without permission, and his legal team has vowed to use the full force of the law to get to the bottom of the matter.

BUT IS IT ART?

Loo paper has been extensively used by prisoners for writing forbidden literature like letters to loved ones, notes and their memoirs. Robben Island was no exception. Madiba confided in *Long Walk to Freedom*:

> Another technique was to write in tiny coded script on toilet paper. The paper was so small and easily hidden that this became a popular way of smuggling out messages. When the authorities discovered a number of these communications they took the extraordinary measure of rationing toilet paper.

Hitler's architect, Albert Speer, incarcerated after the Nuremberg trials, kept a secret diary written mainly on toilet paper which he hid in his shoes until sections could be smuggled out. By the time he was released twenty years later, he had amassed 25 000 pages which he shaped into his book *Spandau: The Secret Diaries*. He did not say what he used instead of the toilet paper.

Bogrolls are also a convenient medium for airing health information. When Jenny worked for the London County Council as a supply teacher in the late Fifties, every perforated sheet in the school toilets commanded: NOW WASH YOUR HANDS PLEASE. Perhaps our HIV/AIDS prevention programmes should consider printing DON'T DO IT WITHOUT A CONDOM on all paperwork destined for public toilets?

Today there's a huge choice of type, colour and design, ranging from dingy unbleached paper for eco-freaks via dainty floral patterns to the gift rolls printed with scatological comments and cartoons that go with such hee-haw items as whoopee cushions and willy warmers. Logos are also popular with large organisations, though they can be expensive. A June 1991 Sapa-Reuter news item read:

SAVING : THE BOTTOM LINE

AMSTERDAM. - KLM Royal Dutch Airlines, which made a 630 million guilder loss in its 1990-91 financial year, has replaced the designer toilet paper used on its aircraft with a plain version to help cut costs. An article in the company's staff journal said KLM was saving 50 000 guilders a year by no longer printing a small aircraft motif on its toilet paper.

Bogrolls seem to have made their mark in the fine art field too. In the June 1984 *Style*, Angela Embleton wrote about Austrian-born local artist Gerhard Batha whose tools of the trade are toilet paper and acrylic paints:

TISSUE OF ARTISTIC FANTASY

Gerhard Batha's grocer must view him with deep suspicion, because every week Batha staggers from his local grocery shop clutching huge armloads of loo paper. He also buys acrylic paints by the box-load... In his studio he squeezes the tubes straight on to the scrunched-up loo paper, brushing aside such mundane items as palette, brushes or palette knife, and then sweeps the paint straight on to the canvas … whoosh! Sometimes he not only applies the paint with lavatory paper but builds up three-dimensional thicknesses of blobby colour with wads of toilet roll.

Complicated and enigmatic. Rich and exciting. Colourful and wild. Those are the adjectives that apply to the big, bold, brilliant paintings of Gerhard Batha.

Fast-forward to London and a report from Dirk de Villiers on March 1 1994 in *The Star Tonight*:

> What do you make of 18 rolls of toilet paper, 315 bars of melted chocolate, and a single hand-turned record player in an otherwise empty 22-metre gallery room? Does the word art come to mind?
>
> You would not be alone in failing to make this connection. Yet that is what the creators of these objects claim for their work.
>
> The rolls of soft white toilet paper assembled by Susan Stockwell are on display at the Bernard Jacobson Gallery in London's elegant Bond Street… 'Untitled' is the title of the toilet paper exhibit, and someone is said to have asked staff at the gallery: 'Will there be a performance?' Only to be informed: 'No, it's just a site-specific installation.' Which means, I'm told, that it is a work created for a particular space. It can be yours for R50 000, if you know what you can do with it.

A few months later in August 1994 Kendell Geers, *enfant terrible* of the Johannesburg art scene, held an exhibition at the Everard Read Contemporary gallery in Rosebank. A somewhat bemused Gillian Anstey reported in the *Sunday Times*:

A South African artist claims to have sold two works
– a stained nude magazine centrespread and a dirty
towel on a rail – for R6 500. The items, by self-
confessed 'con-artist and agent provocateur' Kendell
Geers, have gone to mystery buyers in
Johannesburg... They include the pages from
Hustler magazine, for R3 000, and the towel, which
Geers used to wipe his sweaty face after working in
his studio, for R3 500.

Another work – a toilet roll in a ceramic holder
– is still waiting for a buyer at R2 500.

Comments on the exhibition ranged from:

S A National Gallery director Marilyn Martin's,
'This is not anything new... It is up to the public if
they want to pay for it' ... to Yale Fine Arts graduate
and New York photographer Carolina Salguero's,
'There's a sucker born every minute. Geers's
attitude is self-congratulatory and inane.' ...

Geers replied: 'This is not traditional art that
you can put in your arms and take home like framed
works. The concept in South Africa is brand new.
Already people are writing about my work in
international journals. It's not going to be long
before I break out of the South African mould and
launch my international career. This year alone I
have had five international exhibitions.'

Toilet roll holder manufacturers must be cheering.

Back in July 1984 Evelyn Levison had written in the *Sunday
Express* about a presentation called Mummenschanz at the
Civic Theatre by a trio of mimes, which she called 'an
adventure in theatrical disbelief':

> I was projected into a world inhabited by creatures impossible to identify or define. They appeared, mostly one at a time, crawling, creeping, slithering, some with tiny feet, one with a greedy, grasping tongue, one like a mobile corrugated tube, twisting, curving and turning to play an enchanting ball game with the audience... After interval three figures in black leotards ... related wordless tales, hilarious, moving, joyous and sad. One, that left the stage littered with reams of paper, was the unfolding of a toilet-roll love-tangle...

But is it art? we cry in unison with the rest of the baffled. Is it truly art?

ROCK BOTTOM

The nadir of Jenny's public toilet experience was the cubicle at a Portuguese campsite many years ago where a sign warned in several languages that it was forbidden to flush away used paper. It had to be deposited in the open wooden box by the seat which was full of other people's noisome discards.

The reason for this insanitary practice appears in Gerald Durrell's tales of an unforgettable boyhood on the Greek island of Corfu, *My Family & Other Animals*. After his father had died the family were forced to leave England and find a cheaper place to live; 'Larry' was his older brother Lawrence Durrell, the novelist, who is gently mocked throughout the book for his pretensions...

> 'They seem a helpful crowd,' Larry went on. 'The manager himself shifted my bed nearer the window.'

'He wasn't very helpful when I asked for paper,' said Leslie.

'Paper?' asked Mother. 'What did you want paper for?'

'For the lavatory ... there wasn't any in there,' explained Leslie.

'Shhh! Not at the table,' whispered Mother.

'You obviously don't look,' said Margo in a clear and penetrating voice; 'they've got a little box full by the pan.'

'Margo, dear!' exclaimed Mother, horrified.

'What's the matter? Didn't you see the little box?'

Larry gave a snort of laughter. 'Owing to the somewhat eccentric plumbing system of the town,' he explained to Margo kindly, 'that little box is provided for the ... er ... debris, as it were, when you have finished communing with nature.'

Margo's face turned scarlet with a mixture of embarrassment and disgust. 'You mean ... you mean ... that was ... my God! I might have caught some foul disease,' she wailed, and, bursting into tears, fled from the dining room.

ENDPAPER

While giving a lecture to the University of Cape Town Summer School, it occurred to Tim that there was one great lacuna in English literature. No poem had ever, as far as he knew, been written about a toilet roll. He promptly composed an ode in an afternoon. Like a symphony it has four movements (or seasons), starting briskly, followed by a slower pace, then building to a crescendo. But just when you think it's all over there's an extra movement, which is a surprise. (Rather than a symphony he had wanted to write chamber music, but for that you have to be a little potty).

NB: The original of this deathless poetry is written on very flimsy, perforated, two-ply paper which was smuggled out of the Summer School. It is available for purchase by an American university for a great number of dollars.

EAU DE TOILET ROLL

(For Spenser, Shakespeare, Milton, Marvell, Wordsworth, Shelley, Keats and the staff of the UCT Summer School)

1.

Hail to thee, blithe Spirit! Lovely tree thou wert,
Even if your holder is a bugger to insert.
Perhaps it's no relief for you to be
In here, but oh, the difference to me!

In youth the sweet name of Jeyes is
A kaleidoscope of nightmare glazes:
They stood in rows and stiff, like grease-proof paper,
And didn't so much wipe, as rape yer.

But now you come in different shapes and sizes –
So many colours as the cunning mind devizes.
No motion have I now: the reason why
A slumber does my spirit steal – baby-soft two-ply
Sweet Thames, run softly till I end my song.

2.

Much have I travelled in the realms of old
With you at all times ready to unfold
And drop your petals in the desert night
Unseen by Bedouin or dark Shi'ite.

No idle gossip round the village pumpkin
To see if cob will fit the country bumpkin;
Without you these are faery lands forlorn,
Bereft, like Ruth amongst the alien corn.

When caught in some grotty foreign grotto,
In darkness pent and groping for a motto,
I feel your trusty touch, what can be braver
Than you, Forget-me-not, Twin-saver?
Sweet Thames run softly till I end my song.

3.

Who hath not oft been in the farmhouse loo?
Sometimes we go ha-ha, sometimes boo-hoo.
It's times like these we must not shut the door.
What are these words worth on the granary floor?

Just as the oo-ah bird which pecks the grain,
We come like fowls to make our mark, and strain
To concentrate on what's before, and what's behind –
No matter whether urn or jar – gone with the wind.

If all we do is decompose and deconstruct,
Then surely we are well and truly plucked.
We poets from Cape Town to the Reef
Must ask the question, 'Where's the bloody beef?'
Sweet Thames run softly till I end my song.

4.

But wait! With flighty heart one summer morn
We seat ourselves… and look… and find you gorn.
Gorn! Gorn! The word is like a tolling bell
To one who's caught 'tween purgatory and hell.

They also serve who only sit and shout
For wife or loved one to come and bail you out.
Politer words prevent a huff or fit
Such as, 'No dear, just having a good sit.'

A tactful hand around the door delivers
A ball of paper which becomes, in rivers,
Through her missed aim, beyond your grasp, a wraith:
A small step must become a leap of faith.
Sweet Thames run softly till I end my song.

5.

But now, o love, o star, o steadfast starling,
Skip to the loo, skip to the loo, my darling.
The sun will soon be gone, and time be fleeing;
Soon pulls Almighty God the Chain of Being.

Then must we roll all our strength and all
Our sweetness up into one porc'lain bowl
And tear our pleasures with rough strife
Thorough the leaden pipes of life.

Ah, then, my lovely, would that I were thee
And roll, oh roll, majestic to the sea.
Till then, this humble tribute and no more –
To those great poets who have gone before.
Sweet Thames, run softly now I end my song.

Datta. Dayadhvam. Damyata.
Shantih shantih shantih
(The Peace that passeth understanding)

BY WAY OF ENDING

Boeing had a problem when a number of its 747s kept falling out of the sky when their wings kept coming off. None of the company's technical experts could solve the problem. In desperation they turned to a local South African farmer called Van der Merwe who said he had the solution. He drilled a number of holes in the wings close to the fuselage of each plane. They have never had a problem since. When asked why he had done that, Van der Merwe said, 'They never tear along the perforations.'

In faraway America, Vice-President Dan Quayle (of 'potatoe' fame) had a brainwave in 1990. He presented George Bush with a toilet roll holder that played the presidential anthem, *Hail to the Chief*. (Does everybody have to stand to attention while this is played?)

HORROR
STORIES

Oh dear, what can the matter be?
Two old ladies got locked in the lavatory
They were there from Monday to Saturday
Nobody knew they were there.

Anyone with small children who have discovered how to turn a key or push a bolt knows the scenario: child goes to the toilet, locks the door, then can't unlock it. Panic, specially if it's upstairs. The child is sobbing bitterly, the tiny window is burglar-barred, the key or the bolt has jammed and the locksmith is out on another job...

Stories about being locked in the loo are legion, but few incarcerations are as pragmatically handled as the one Jilly Cooper writes about in *Class*:

> In very grand houses they have an estate carpenter permanently on the premises doing repairs. One friend got locked in the lavatory when she was staying in Yorkshire, and her host fed her Bloody Marys through the keyhole with a straw while they waited for the house carpenter to come and free her.

An Edwardian woman's comforter had his mind on higher things. Gwen Raverat in *Period Piece* talks of the 'three celebrated improper' stories her Uncle Lenny used to tell her:

> The one I liked best was about a lady who got locked into the lavatory on a Sunday morning; so her brother-in-law, a clergyman, sat on a chair up against the door and read the morning service aloud to her from outside.

Jenny's toilet door began to stick last year during the rains, trapping a lunch guest whose shouts for help didn't reach the rest of the party who had walked down to the bottom of the garden. Fortunately, Charlotte had her cellphone in her handbag and they heard the telephone ringing...

The infernal accessory has its uses.

Being trapped by the U-bend itself was the fate of an unwary traveller in February 1993:

> PARIS. - A man brought a French high speed train to a halt on Sunday when his hand got stuck down a lavatory. The hapless passenger had been trying to retrieve his wallet, which had fallen into the bowl. He sounded the alarm and the train stopped. Firemen with metal cutters extricated him – and the toilet. TV showed him on the platform with the bowl around his arm.

He was more fortunate than poor Bokkie Gerber, a *Rapport* journalist. On 29 July 1984, Jack Dewes reported in the *Sunday Times*:

> A late night trip to the lavatory nearly cost sports journalist Bokkie Gerber his life. The toilet bowl in his hotel room broke under him and his back was severely gashed.
>
> He managed to get to the telephone and call an ambulance but he was close to bleeding to death by the time they got him to hospital for emergency surgery.

FLASHES IN THE PAN

Improperly ventilated sewerage systems are notorious for build-ups of methane gas, sometimes with incendiary results. In October 1991 there were two reports of exploding toilets. A *Business Day* snippet read:

> A public toilet in Beijing has exploded, spewing a fireball skyward. Residents saw an old woman scrambling out from the women's side and a young man running from the other side. Both suffered burns in the blast, which was believed to have been caused by a build-up of methane gas.

Eleven days later, Associated Press captioned a photograph showing a woman sitting next to a toilet in smithereens:

> Dutch housewife Miriam Smeeke shows the damage to her bathroom after her toilet exploded this week. It was the second time in two years that the family toilet had been blasted by an explosion in Arnhem's sewerage system. There were no injuries in either explosion. Dutch Environment Police are investigating whether explosives are being discharged into the sewers from an industrial area nearby.

In May 1997 it happened again in Sanford, Florida. Correspondents for Sapa-DPA clearly enjoyed composing their newsflash:

> A Florida man had an uplifting experience in a toilet at the Seminole County Courthouse here this

week. Officials said the man, whose name was not released in order to save him further embarrassment, was in the toilet on Wednesday when the pan he was sitting on blew up. They blamed a firehose pressure test elsewhere in the building.

Courthouse staffers said this was the second time a toilet had exploded there in the past two years. The victim suffered no injuries, except to his dignity.

DESCENDING FORTUNES

People are always dropping things down loos. As early as 1771, an exasperated Englishman called Sylas Neville wrote in his diary:

> Had a fine accident, going into the little-house ten guineas which I had put into my watch-pocket on the left side dropped out while I sat. 4 of them fell into the vault. Was obliged to send for a carpenter & have the seat taken up... At last all were found, tho' I had given over 2 of them. More lucky in getting over this accident than I am commonly, God be praised. He knows I could ill afford to lose a guinea.

ACADEMIC VAPOURS

Vera Stravinsky once found something dubious in Auden's lavatory and flushed down the loo what turned out to have been the sweet course, cooling. Bathrooms and kitchens merge bizarrely in Wittgenstein's case, too, except that with him it was an insistence on doing the dishes in the bathtub...

At Trinity, Cambridge, Wittgenstein had rooms (with no private lavatory) over A E Housman, the great classical scholar and poet – also homosexual, austere, perfectionist and deeply divided. When Wittgenstein had an attack of diarrhoea he tried to save himself the perilous trip across Whewell's Court by asking, through his bed maker, if he might make use of Housman's convenience. But the reply came back that Housman was a philosophical hedonist and therefore refused the request.

– From a review of the film Wittgenstein *by Paul Taylor in the* Independent, *24 March 1993*

Of all the objects that have been flushed away by mistake, the next two must be the oddest...

Arthur Goldstuck, computer fundi and purveyor of urban legends, had a regular slot in the *Weekly Mail* called S'True Eksê which carried 'true tales from around South Africa'. Topping the first one in February 1993 was:

EYE-TISHOO

A one-eyed Pietermaritzburg man arrived at the Darvill sewerage works outside the city with a desperate appeal: had anyone seen his glass eye?

'Apparently the man flushed the toilet as he was blowing his nose,' said an official at the sewerage works. 'The glass eye suddenly shot out and disappeared down the toilet bowl.'

The official said the chances of finding lost items during the purification process were slim, but they 'would keep an eye out' for the missing object.

Rejected males are sometimes driven to appalling deeds. Melody McDougall of *The Star's* Vereeniging Bureau reported in November 1992:

An attractive Vereeniging woman lost part of her right ear when a former boyfriend allegedly bit off a piece and tossed it into a toilet during a fight.

Elize Steinberg … intends suing the man for pain and suffering. Speaking from her Joubert Street home yesterday, she said the drama occurred about three weeks ago during a fight. She locked herself and her two daughters in a bedroom, but the man kicked down the door. 'He sat on top of me and then bit off a piece of my ear.'

He later flushed the piece of flesh down a toilet. She underwent an emergency operation the same night but was informed that the damaged ear would have to be reconstructed with plastic surgery.

Police are investigating.

FLIGHT FRIGHTS

Horror stories about plane toilets are nothing new. The first one adds fuel to all those fearsome tales one used to hear about being sucked out.

Martha Gellhorn was an intrepid and gifted war correspondent. She met Ernest Hemingway during the Spanish war in the thirties and became his third wife – the only one who left him. He kept all her belongings and called her a 'wicked wild bitch'; she said, 'He was cruel – in words – given to unpredictable murdering of people who had thought he was their buddy,' and later, 'I would grow old but never grow wise.' She visited South Africa shortly before she died in her late eighties, still working.

In a book of reminiscences called *Travels With Myself and Another* (the other being a grumpy Hemingway), she wrote of a hell run in China:

> I left Hongkong alone to fly via Chungking and Kunming to Lashio, the Burma end of the Burma Road, and returned immediately the same way, material for a Collier's article. The airline, called China National Aviation Company, consisted of 2 DC3s and 3 DC2s, elderly machines and no nonsense about comfort. Compared to passenger planes now, these were flying beetles. The floor sloped steeply, the chairs were canvas on metal frames, the toilet, behind a green curtain, gave a small circular view of the ground below.

Even modern planes are not as hermetically sealed as we imagine. A small news item in June 1989 read:

> VANCOUVER. - Leaking aircraft lavatories are creating a storm of controversy in parts of Canada and the US. Four times in recent weeks there have been reports of large chunks of ice falling to the ground from passenger jets. The Canadian Aviation Safety Board suspects leaking loos aboard planes are causing urine and water to freeze on the outside of aircraft at high altitudes. When the planes descend, the ice starts to melt and falls away.

Being locked in up there can be expensive as well as embarrassing. *The Star* Bureau reported from London in June 1987:

> It was the moment every seasoned airline traveller dreads. When he should have been fastening his seatbelt for landing, a man on a British Airways flight from London to Manchester this week found himself locked in the plane's toilet.
>
> As the Boeing 757 was preparing to land, the cabin crew carried out their usual head count and found they were one short. They soon realised where the missing passenger was and told the pilot to keep on flying. The highly embarrassed passenger eventually emerged and the plane landed 16 minutes late.

With Mile High Club membership apparently on the increase, few will be surprised by the small paragraph in the *Sunday Times* in March 1987:

> A couple's mid-air sex session in a jetliner's loo gave other passengers a quick flash. For, as the couple moved, they bumped the emergency loo light on and off.
>
> A stewardess saw the flashing light and used a spare key to open the loo door on the Spain to Manchester flight. A passenger said, 'She then ran red-faced down the aisle.'

(We do not believe that 'making love' in an aircraft toilet is possible nowadays since all are fitted with smoke detectors which would surely be triggered in such situations.)

THE ULTIMATE HORROR

There was a young fellow named Hyde
Who fell down a privy and died.
His unfortunate brother
Then fell down another,
And now they're interred side by side.

This is by no means a rare accident where old cesspits are still in use. Wood rots, corrugated iron rusts, mud brick crumbles, and unwary stumblers are at risk of precipitation into the ultimate horror.

In mid-nineteenth century England when sanitary reform was a hot topic, *The Builder* reported a 'terrible incident' in March 1845:

On the 17th instant, an accident of the most appalling nature occurred in the Female Penitentiary, Exeter. Twenty-one of the inmates retired for a short time to a small room but little frequented, for the purpose of allowing the committee to inspect the apartment they usually occupied, when the floor of the room instantly gave away, and twenty of the unfortunates were immersed in the pestilential contents of an ancient cesspit underneath, the other one supporting herself on a part of the floor still remaining.

The cries and appeals of assistance soon brought to their aid the committee, who succeeded in releasing the woman sustaining herself on the broken part of the floor, from her perilous situation and dragging the others from the pit. In five of these however, we regret to say, life was extinct.

(Quoted in Lucinda Lambton's *Temples of Convenience*)

Newborn babies have an extraordinary ability to survive even when abandoned in horrifying circumstances by desperate mothers. Since some women give birth suddenly and without notice, it is not unusual for it to happen in a toilet. In August 1990, a desperate 20-year-old student teacher at a Venda training college gave birth to a child who fell or was thrown into a long-drop. *The Star* reported:

> Apparently the infant's wails alerted neighbours to its presence in the pit last Sunday morning, after the baby had spent the night in the foul-smelling pit. They immediately called the police ... (and the toilet was) demolished brick by brick. Then police lowered the mother into the pit with ropes tied around her waist... The baby was rushed to Tshilidzini Hospital but died seven hours later...
>
> According to medical experts, the infant may have survived for as long as it did because its body weight would not yet have been sufficient to drag it under the dense contents of the toilet. Records show newborn babies being able to cling to life under some of the most difficult circumstances. An infant's ability to survive would depend on a number of factors, including the gestational period and blood glucose levels at the time of birth and soon after.

A German baby's entry into the world was equally disastrous, though he survived the ordeal. A short piece in *Time* magazine on 2 May 1994 read:

DIPPOLDISWALDE: A newborn baby's remarkable arrival – and survival – have delighted residents of this village in Germany. The child's mother, identified only as Manja P, was seated on the toilet last Tuesday when she suddenly found herself giving birth.

When the umbilical cord parted, the baby, a boy, slid down the 40cm-wide drainage pipe of the old-fashioned waterless toilet. Firemen called by Maja's husband carefully opened the pipe ... and found the baby 45 minutes later, whimpering but alive. 'It was enormous luck that the baby got stuck where it did,' marvelled the fire chief. 'Otherwise he would have drowned in the septic tank.'

At last report mother and baby Michael were doing well.

An even more remarkable survivor was the baby born in the toilet of a Chinese train in May 1999. Sapa-AP's dispatch gave the details:

BEIJING. - A newborn survived a fall through the toilet of a Chinese train, escaping with only cuts and bruises after falling on to the rails.

The boy's mother, Yang Zhu, was going home by train on May 4 to give birth when she began to suffer stomach pains... Her husband took her to the washroom where, 'to her great surprise', she gave birth in the toilet 'as soon as she squatted down.'

Yang panicked, ripped off the umbilical cord, and the baby slipped down through the toilet and fell on to the rails. Guards spotted the baby, but before they could reach him, another train sped right over him.

The guards took the infant to a hospital, where he was found to have just a small cut to the head and slight bruises.

> **Gustave Flaubert (1850):** From time to time, I open a newspaper. Things seem to be proceeding at a dizzy rate. We are dancing not on the edge of a volcano, but on the wooden seat of a latrine, and it seems to me more than a touch rotten. Soon society will go plummeting down and drown in nineteen centuries of shit. There'll be quite a lot of shouting.

THE ARACHNID THREAT ...

If snakes are a problem in vulnerable lavatories (see LONG-DROPS), so are spiders. Australian Clive James wrote, again in *Unreliable Memoirs*:

> The real horror among spiders was more likely to be encountered in the lavatory itself. This was the red-back. The red-back is mainly black, with a scarlet stripe down where its spine would be if it were a vertebrate. Looking like a neatly rigged and painted single-seater that might once have been flown by von Richthofen, the red-back had enough poison in it to immobilise a horse. It had the awkward habit, in unsewered areas like ours, of lurking under the lavatory seat. If a red-back bit you on the behind you were left with the problem of where to put the tourniquet and not long to think about it. Nor could you ask anyone to suck out the poison, unless you knew them very well indeed.

GRAND FINALE

The most bizarre horror story of all started doing the rounds ten years ago and still serves as a useful admonition not to buy food of dubious provenance. *The Star* reported on 7 July 1989:

> DURBAN. - Holidaymakers coming to the Natal South Coast were warned today not to buy crayfish from illegal roadside dealers who are going underground in the worst possible way. The sellers have established crayfish 'farms' in bush latrines, the Natal Parks Board warned today.
>
> Parks Board public relations officer Ms June Payn said: 'Crayfish feed quite happily on human excreta as they are filter feeders. After being caught, they are washed in muddy water and put in the latrine pits. Then when the time to sell is right, they are taken out, washed again in the muddy stream and offered for sale at the side of the road. I am surprised that people who have bought crayfish from the roadside have not been poisoned.'
>
> She said anyone who did buy crayfish should ensure the creatures were live to reduce the risk of being poisoned.

(The suggestion that this horrid rumour was put about by Natal residents trying to protect their marine life from predatory up-country visitors is completely false.)

FOR THOSE IN
PERIL ON THE SEAT

173

Few people have associated plumbers with courage. But they have not only changed history, they have also braved it. Tim read somewhere that ten thousand accidents occur in English bathrooms annually, not to mention the dread diseases (cholera, typhoid, dysentery, gastroenteritis) that lurk in the sewers of the world. Despite these dangers, many a plumber, unsuspecting of the noxious and toxic gases, has peered into a recalcitrant cesspit with a lighted match and blown himself to Kingdom Come – or beyond.

They have their moments, however. The following limerick is a joint favourite:

There was a young plumber from Leigh
Who was plumbing a maid by the sea:
Said the maid, 'Cease your plumbing,
I can hear someone coming.'
Said the plumber, still plumbing, 'It's me.'

The historical researcher into loos is not immune to danger either. Tim has often wondered how his own actions have been perceived when he used to take people on social history tours of Johannesburg. One of the mandatory stops was at the Fordsburg Men's Toilet to see the urinals with their bullet-holes from the 1922 Revolt. The furtive shapes of several females being sneaked in for a quick peek might well be recorded in the notebooks of the Vice Squad or Special Branch who were sometimes following. Goodness knows what they thought was going on.

There are also *political dangers*. In his biography of Winston Churchill, William Manchester tells this story. The Labour Prime Minister Clement Attlee met the then Leader of the Opposition in the House Men's Room:

> Attlee, arriving first, had stepped up to the urinal trough when Churchill strode in on the same mission and stood at the trough as far away from him as possible. Attlee said, 'Feeling standoffish today, are we, Winston?' Churchill said, 'That's right. Every time you see something this big, you want to nationalise it.'

There is always, too, potential for *legal disasters*. Stephen Tumim in his book *Great Legal Disasters* quotes Lord Campbell, writing about the lives of the Chief Justices in the 1850s:

> In those days retiring-rooms for the use of the judges were unknown, and a porcelain vase, with a handle to it, was placed in a corner of the court at the extremity of the bench. In the King's Bench at Guildhall the students' box (in which I myself have often sat) was very near this corner.
>
> One day a student who was taking notes, finding the ink in his little ink-bottle very thick, used the freedom secretly to discharge the whole of it into My Lord's porcelain vase. His Lordship soon after having occasion to come to this corner, he was observed in the course of a few moments to become much disconcerted and distressed. In truth, discovering the liquid with which he was filling the vase to be of a jet-black colour, he thought the secretion indicated the sudden attack of some mortal disorder.
>
> In great confusion and anguish of mind he returned to his seat and attempted to resume the trial of the cause but, finding his hand to shake so much that he could not write, he said that on account of an indisposition he was obliged to adjourn the court.

As he was led to his carriage by his servants, the luckless student came up and said to him, 'My Lord, I hope your Lordship will excuse me, as I suspect that I am unfortunately the cause of Your Lordship's apprehensions.' He then described what he had done, expressing deep contrition for his thoughtlessness and impertinence, and saying that he considered it his duty to relieve His Lordship's mind by his confession. Lord Kenyon: 'Sir, you are a man of sense and a gentleman – dine with us on Sunday.'

Lord Ellenborough pursued the same practice. I myself have often heard his large seals dangling from his watch-chain rattle against the vase, as he took in his hand coram populo, decorously turning his back upon them.

Finally, there are *professional and social* dangers, too. Witness the experience of Wallace Deuel which he described in the Chicago *Daily News*, 10 January 1941 (as quoted in Irving J Lee's *Language Habits in Human Affairs*). Deuel was a young doctor called out to visit a rich patient:

Any doctor would have been glad to be called to this house, one of the most beautiful old homes in the city. I felt that my standing in the community was at stake and that it was an important moment.

At the conclusion of the examination I wanted to talk privately with the stiffly starched and immaculate nurse who was in attendance, who, too, was apparently making every effort to be perfect in her professional attitude. I wanted to give some instructions to the nurse and asked the family to excuse us for a moment while I talked to her privately. The nearest and most obvious place was the old-fashioned bathroom adjoining and I asked her to go in. I closed the door.

'Sit down,' I said pointing to the bathroom stool, and then, as she took it, I noticed that the only place left for me was the indispensable one in any bathroom, which was covered by a gold and white lid.

I seated myself and talked for several minutes while the family waited anxiously outside for the verdict. Finally she rose and as I, too, rose, my hand automatically grasped the ornate pear-shaped knob at the end of the chain hanging beside me – and I pulled.

Why I pulled the cursed thing I'll never know except, of course, from force of habit. Instantly the place resounded with the familiar screeches and hisses of flushing water.

'Oh doctor!' she gasped, 'what will they think? – And the door shut! – What can I do?'

'Hell, woman,' I said, my dignity ruined, 'don't ask me what you can do. I don't even know what I can do!'

I was never asked to return.

Bathrooms aren't all perilous places, though. To end this chapter on an upbeat note, we bring you Daisy Ashford's idea of a leisurely morning. Victorian Daisy was nine when she wrote *The Young Visiters* in pencil in a tuppeny notebook; though her intentions were clearly serious, it's become a classic of British humour. In this extract, the heroine Ethel Monticue and her friend Alf Salteena have gone to stay with the wealthy Bernard:

Mr Salteena woke up rarther early next day and was supprised and delighted to find Horace the footman entering with a cup of tea.

Oh thankyou my man said Mr Salteena rolling over in the costly bed. Mr Clark is nearly out of the bath sir announced Horace I will have great plesure in turning it on for you if such is your desire. Well yes you might said Mr Salteena seeing it was the idear and Horace gave a profound bow.

Ethel are you getting up shouted Mr Salteena.

Very nearly replied Ethel faintly from the next room.

I say said Mr Salteena excitedly I have had some tea in bed.

So have I replied Ethel.

Then Mr Salteena got into a mouve dressing goun with yellaw tassles and siezing his soap he wandered off to the bath room which was sumpshous. It had a lovly white shiny bath and sparkling taps and several towels arrayed in readiness by thourghtful Horace. It also had a step for climbing up the bath and other good dodges of a rich nature. Mr Salteena washed himself well and felt very much better.

AFRICANA

Africa's main claim to fame in the matter of waste disposal rests on the shiny carapace of the dung beetle. So good is this enthusiastic insect at keeping the South African veld in optimum condition that we export them to other countries in need – notably Australia.

Dung beetles use fresh dung as a repository for their eggs, either cutting it out of the pat and compacting it into a ball which is rolled away and buried, or excavating a hole beneath the pat which is packed with dung. Once laid, the eggs are kept warm and snug by the fermentation and the hatched larvae – white humped grubs – gobble out hollow cells in which they pupate.

In the process, the beetles break down and distribute the dung and the seeds it contains, fertilising and stimulating plant growth, and tunnel into the soil which improves its porosity and water permeability. Loam soil which has been worked over by dung beetles absorbs five times more water before saturation point is reached than unworked soil, which checks erosion. So it's a useful creature indeed.

If you've read Sir Percy Fitzpatrick's *Jock of the Bushveld* in its original form, you'll know Caldwell's original margin illustrations included a famous blaps: one of the dung beetles was shown pushing a ball of dung with its front legs when everyone knew they used their hind legs. According to Dr Adrian Davis, an entomologist at Pretoria University, this is not strictly true. There are a few species that roll their dung balls in pairs, one pushing and one pulling.

They have a fine-tuned sense of smell too. One of Jenny's brothers was on the team of surveyors who worked on the triangulation of Botswana, camping in remote areas, and he has kept people in fits for years with his imitation of a dung beetle. He swears that when a camper grabbed a spade and headed for the nearest clump of scraggly bushes, the beetles would home in from miles around, dive-bombing the unhappy sitter in their rush to get at a fresh supply.

DUNG BEETLES DOWN UNDER

Although Australia has 250 species of dung beetles, they are adapted to kangaroo dung. When cows and sheep were introduced the local beetles couldn't cope, dung covered the pastures, buffalo fly maggots moved in and the fly population became uncontrollable. (Hence the traditional hat with the corks!)

South Africa has about 650 species of dung beetles and it was suggested that some of these be tried. Dr Davis recounts that in the 1970s entomologists collected and surface-sterilised the eggs of species they thought would be suitable, placed them in artificial broods and flew them to Australia. After two generations in quarantine they were taken out, bred once more and the then third generation was released. Many of the eggs died, as did beetles that were not matched with the correct climate and habitats. But some of the more generous species have now spread over large portions of northern Australia, aided initially by farmhands who shovelled little pats of dung off the back of their 'utes' in areas where the beetles were breeding, waited until eggs had been laid, then scooped the gravid pats up again to spread further afield.

The fly maggots' food supply soon dwindled and Oz farmers were so delighted that they even gave dung beetles to each other as gifts.

PRAWN TALES

Parktown Prawns are insects of quite a different order: terrifyingly ugly and threatening giant crickets that inhabit Gauteng homes and gardens, and have a nasty habit of crawling out of hiding at unexpected moments. They jump at you, they exude a revolting smell and they're almost impossible to catch and kill.

Gauteng residents are always on the lookout for foolproof methods of dealing with the beasts, murder being favoured. Chris Campling, a journalist long lost to London, gave his in a *Star Review* column way back in July 1984:

PARKTOWN PRAWNS MEET THEIR WATERLOO

It's a lesson every Johannesburger living within the Prawn belt learned at his mother's knee: never squash a Parkie, because they stink. Instead, you drown them.

All very well in theory, but there are few things more pitiful than watching a grown man (me) chasing an insect the size of a small dog with an upended glass and a magazine... Eventually, however, even a Prawn must get tired out, and that is when you pounce. Glass over the Prawn, magazine slid carefully over the opening, and a triumphant trip to the loo to flush the thing away...

Unfortunately, Parktown Prawns can all swim like Mark Spitz. After each successive flush, an unearthly calm would descend until, in a scene reminiscent of the Sorcerer's Apprentice sequence from Fantasia, the Prawn would begin to climb up the bowl. What it intended to do once it made it back to safety I have no idea. Probably rip my throat out. Anyway, I never bothered to find out.

Wad after wad of toilet paper would be heaped on to the mighty midget. Flush would follow flush until, finally, blessed release. No more Prawn.

PINKY-PINKY

A beast of quite a different order to Parktown Prawns threatened Gauteng schools at the beginning of November 1994, as told by Shirley Woodgate in *The Star:*

It's short, it lives in a toilet, its name is Pinky-Pinky, and fear of the half-human, half animal apparition has swept PWV township schools. It surfaced north of Pretoria last week and Moretele Primary School children described it to Mamelodi police officer Lieutenant Elias Mawela.

They say it has a face divided in four parts: male on one side, female on the other, with the forehead and nose of a cat and the mouth and chin of a baby or snake. Pinky-Pinky likes girls with pink panties, wears a dress on one leg and narrow trousers on the other, and sways its hips to and fro in a curious dancing motion.

The investigating officer was told the ghost never appeared to adults and was mostly a friendly spirit, although one young boy claimed it had slapped him and stolen his socks.

Mawela stood outside the toilets while the youngsters chanted the schoolground ditty: 'My name is Pinky-Pinky, I live in the toilet, my father is a sangoma and my mother is a witch', in order to lure the apparition out. But the pupils ran out screaming hysterically before he got a glimpse of the being. Mawela said he had closed his file on the case.

RAU anthropologist Dr Kees van der Waal said academics took such appearances seriously, particularly as they were often a valve for the release of social stress – in this case, probably pupils' end-of-year exams.

BAOBABBALOO

Ten years earlier in 1984, the level of social stress was far worse: the country was in turmoil, people were angry and afraid, and young white men were still being conscripted and sent up to the border to fight an unjust and brutal war. However, there was an island of calm in the Caprivi, a *Star* correspondent reported from Pietersburg:

> ...where you awake at dawn to the call of the fish eagle and the grunts of hippos in the Zambezi, (and) it is difficult to believe you are in a war zone. This strip of land, sandwiched between Angola, Zambia, Zimbabwe and Botswana, has an abundance of wildlife. Just down the road from Katima Mulilo, military headquarters for the Eastern Caprivi, you are likely to meet a herd of elephant or buffalo. The village itself has one of Southern Africa's most unique tourist attractions: a toilet in a baobab tree.
>
> Would other trees grow as big with a permanent supply of fresh fertiliser?

The Star ran an editorial on 13 March 1986 that was a good example of the frequent use by the media of lavatorial words and images:

CHAIN REACTION

What a relief that the State Security Council was able to find out through its network of Joint Management Centres that a shortage of lavatories can cause internal disturbances. General Malan cited such an instance in an interview aimed at dispelling the bad odour attached to the State's elaborate security management system. He reported that when a JMC had identified the problem, the Security Council set in motion a train of overt actions that quickly eased the pressure. In the main we agree with the general – it is advisable to flush out the problems in situ.

That accommodating baobab would have been taxed in Simon's Town. John Scott, now deputy editor of the *Cape Times*, has been writing his P.S. column for decades. On 1 December 1973 he noted:

> The Simon's Town Municipality has found financial relief in the smallest room of the house. It has decided to impose a lavatory tax of R24 a year on every house which possesses one. Householders who pretend they do without are in for a rude shock. Municipal inspectors will flush them out.

The Municipality apparently needed the funds to pay for a new sewerage system:

> Some people may resent having to pay as much for their bowel movements as for their car licences, and could try to unseat the council in a motion of censure. Even the feudal barons of old, who taxed their serfs on everything they produced, including children, didn't think of imposing a latrine levy.
>
> But of course the Council's tax is very reasonable when you work it out. If you use the toilet only once a day, R24 a year amounts to only 6½c a time, a cheap price to pay for instant relief. This figure is bound to be even lower. For other members of the household will also be in and out constantly. Laxatives will enable the whole family to get its money's worth. The more you go, the more you save. Unfortunately this is where the constipated ratepayers of Simon's Town lose out...

CAPE TOWN CAPERS

There were several selections of the best of John Scott's P.S. columns, which kept a humorous eye on municipal affairs and the quirks of Capetonians. Three pieces from *Where's All the White Air Gone?* deserve a wider airing – in more ways than one.

On 9 October 1975 he wrote about the new scheme that was to recycle waste water from Cape Flats sewage into drinking water, reporting the reactions of Windhoek people in 1969 when it became the first centre in the world to add recycled water to the public supply:

> I lived there a few years earlier when they opened the pilot plant. Never was a town so torn in half by conflicting emotions. On one hand it was speechless with pride at being the world's first to drink its own sewage.
>
> Visitors to the plant were offered a glass of the recycled liquid as though it were very old KWV, to be sipped and savoured. Actually it was quite tasteless and could be drunk without difficulty as long as you kept your thoughts in check.
>
> On the other hand the town was swept by a wave of revulsion... After the switch-over, consumption of beer rose to unimagined heights.

On 12 August 1976 he wrote a piece about an architectural booboo:

ATHLETICS IN THE SURGEONS' LOO

The new R2½ million wing of the Somerset Hospital, Green Point ... has everything that opens and shuts except the doors of the surgeons' lavatories in the operating theatre suites... The door is on one side of the cubicle, opens inwards and shaves the toilet bowl by one centimetre...

There are two ways of shutting the door once you are inside. You can either do right-angle splits over the toilet seat with your feet wedged against each wall ...or you can climb on to the seat, shut the door from an elevated position, and climb down again.

Said my surgical guide, 'Some of my colleagues are not as young or as slim as they used to be. They totter about on top of that seat like mountaineers fighting a high wind. One day there's going to be a disaster.'

The problem was solved by re-hanging the doors to open outwards.

One week later on 19 August, John highlighted the noisome existence of the nearby Green Point outfall pipe:

UP TO THE NECK IN WATER, SORTA

One of the compensations of living in a densely-populated city is that whatever worries you may have about the quality of life around you, there is always an expert offering reassurance. I was pleased, therefore, to hear from ... the City Engineer and ... the Medical Officer of Health that the outflow of 35 megalitres of raw sewage a day into the sea at Green Point represents a negligible threat to health. One megalitre equals a million litres, which just shows you how little it is compared to the Atlantic Ocean.

However, there has been some disquieting evidence that not all of this sewage sinks respectfully to the bed of the Cape Basin ... midway between us and Tristan da Cunha. Some of it ends up slopping about the Green Point rockpools and coming ashore at nearby beaches...

The experts say that sewage washback on to rocks and beaches only occurs in certain wind and tide conditions. All you have to do before taking the family to Green Point beach is to find out which wind and tide conditions turn the rockpools into cesspools.

Green Point is not the only beach on the South Atlantic plagued by sewage washback. A friend of Jenny's who fortunately found a space big enough to spread her towel out on Copacabana Beach found herself sharing the waves with solid evidence from Rio's sewerage system. Her only consolation was that when she hurried out of the sea to find a shower, the towel was still there.

LIVING UP TO HIS NAME

Kenya-based archaeologist and wildlife expert Richard Leakey gave a talk recently at Cape Town's Baxter Theatre. According to a member of the audience, Leakey forgot to turn off his throat mike when he went to the toilet. As a result, the assembly was treated to the sound of zipper being pulled, liquid hitting porcelain, then zipper being pulled again – all in stereo.

– From the *Financial Mail*, 31 January 1992

STAYING WITH SEWAGE...

Denis Beckett's feisty *Frontline* was in its infancy in 1985 when Natal journalist David Basckin had a regular column called Durban Poison. In April of that year he wrote about an experience all householders dread: a blocked toilet. There was help at hand, though, from...

THE LAUGHING SEWER MEN

Not only would (the toilet) not flush but it appeared to be working in reverse. Like a horror movie running backwards, like long-forgotten nightmares thrusting themselves into unwelcome consciousness, like the undead of some voodoo rite rising from their graves, the demonic denizens of the sewer came floating hideously into view.

I dropped the lid like a man possessed and fled the bathroom. The lady on the telephone was very nice. 'Not to worry, Mr Biscuit,' she said, 'our sewer men will come right away. They're radio-controlled and on 24-hour standby.' Leaving me with images of bionic plumbers, she rang off.

Exactly 37 minutes later the tiny cul-de-sac outside our house was filled with a giant yellow Corporation truck with SANITATION on the doors. Accompanying Mr Pillay, the driver, were nine workers in jolly orange day-glow overalls...

'Blocked toilet, eh?' said Mr Pillay. 'Not to worry, we'll have it clear in no time.' Issuing a quick series of instructions he set the men to work. There was a great air of efficiency and bustle. Working briskly and cheerfully, the men unrolled a drain rod and began the practice of their dark and magical art.

Night fell. The clanging of manhole lids and the rhythmic squooshing of the drain plunger thundered on. But the sewer remained recalcitrant. Puzzled, the sewer men fell into discussion... The answer, after a fair amount of laughter, was The Screw. Plunged into the hellish depths of the sewer it threaded itself into Whatever Was Blocking the Pipe. Out it came to the cheers of the sewer men. I looked away. There's a limit to what a sensitive chap can handle.

While the men cheerfully loaded the instruments of their trade onto the truck I signed the invoice

Mr Pillay offered me. 'Happy lot,' I commented. 'Very happy,' said Mr Pillay, 'very happy indeed.'

As the truck drove off leaving behind a faint smell of Jeyes Fluid another perfume attracted my attention. It was like tobacco, only more so. And it came from the unusually thick hand-rolled cigarettes that the laughing sewer men were so joyously smoking.

The idea of radio-controlled plumbers reminds Tim of a scheme he had a while ago. Two of his children studied law and he envisaged setting them up in a van which would rove the city streets. Subscribers in need of a lawyer – an aged relative threatening to die intestate or a couple in desperate need of a divorce after midnight – could get instant response. A row of panic buttons in the home could answer all emergencies: a paramedic, a paramilitiaman, a lawyer, a plumber.

A NEW ICE AGE

The toilet habits of the rich and famous are not a usual subject for discussion among this newspaper's staff, but this week it was irresistible. A Cobbleigh colleague visiting the Palace at Sol's Lost City returned with the weird news that the men's urinals were filled with blocks of ice which melted on contact. That's about as much detail as Cobbleigh is prepared to go into. But why the ice? Surely we should be told.

Thomas Cobbleigh in the *Sunday Times Diary*, 24 April 1994

TAKE A SEAT

Back in 1988 one of Barry Ronge's winter columns in the *Sunday Times Magazine* described the loo seat as the coldest substance known to man.

A few columns later, on August 28, he reported on the wide response he had received:

One generous soul even sent me a pristine white object she described as a 'tochus-warmer', a soft and snuggly furry job which fitted over the seat and did what its name implied. I was prevented from using it, however, because whenever I looked at it I was overwhelmed by its value as a metaphor for present-day South Africa – very soft, very white and constantly being sat upon by various bums with dubious intentions...

The same column also elicited a sparkly blue oval cut-out not unlike sponge, which you are supposed to gum onto the seat for comfort. There was even a knitting pattern for a seat, a seat cover and, goodness me, even a little woollen poodle in the belly of which a spare loo-roll could nestle...

The point is that my single lament produced about 10 wonderful solutions to the bathroom chill factor... It also made me realise just how many pampered bums there are in South Africa, something I never considered before, although when you think carefully about it, it is self-evident.

Anyway, the rest of the world seems to have spotted it which is why they call for sanctions, boycotts and other punitive measures. And when you consider the bums they are thinking about, you realise that a plush toilet seat is not the answer. A swift kick might be a much better idea.

(NB For more on seat-warming, read Roald Dahl's piece about a fag's duties in NOSTALGIA.)

SPITTING IMAGE OF A WORLD CHAMP

South Africa's new buckdung spitting champion is Nylstroom's Stoffel Niewoudt, who spat a piece of buckdung over a distance of 13.39m during the Waterberg Tourism Festival at Nylstroom last Saturday. That was 2cm further than the runner-up, Eddie Kelbrick, who won the contest last year. Kelbrick still holds the world record of 13.8m. The women's championship was won this year by Kelbrick's sister, Chrisna Kelbrick, who spat a piece of buckdung 9.45m.

– Reported by Arthur Goldstuck in the *Weekly Mail & Guardian*, 3 June 1994.

THAT AMAZING ELECTION

1994 was the year of our first democratic election with its potent icon of a rainbow flag fluttering under the fly-past helicopters. In the throes of our current alarm about rising crime, we have forgotten too easily the violence and killing and the atmosphere of gloom and doom and panic hoarding that preceded it. Here is a salutary little reminder from Inside Track by 'Hector Sauer' in the *Saturday Star* of 19 March 1994:

> *Die Afrikaner*, mouthpiece of Jaap Marais's small Herstigte Nasionale Party, thought of everything giving a list of precautions to be taken and supplies to be stored in case of an unspecified 'emergency situation'.
>
> 'A chemical toilet of the type used in caravans should be available if there is any possibility that your supply of water could be cut off. In addition, keep a chamber pot handy so it can be emptied out

of the window should there be no other way of dealing with the situation.'

Not the best way to make friends, especially if you live in a flat – unless 'the enemy' happens to be passing by at the same time.

Irrepressible as always, Carol Lazar found herself on election night in a car with a volunteer driver, an IEC monitor and 12 ballot boxes in the mother of all traffic jams outside Nasrec, where votes would be counted. In the *Weekend Star* of April 30 her report appeared under the heading:

NEVER MIND THE BALLOTS, JUST WHERE CAN WE PEE?

The line of drivers waiting to disgorge ballot boxes from the PWV was endless. I counted 157 in the immediate vicinity... The line crept slowly and the bladders of ballot box transporters, unprepared for a long wait, swelled agonisingly. 'A toilet, a toilet, my ballot boxes for a toilet,' muttered Oliver.

A deep trench beside the road was discovered and people climbed through the thin barbed-wire fence in order to companionably relieve themselves.

Everything became a group effort. Somebody 50 cars ahead found a toilet in the Nasrec building. No matter that it was pitch dark, that the lights didn't work, that a soldier with an assault rifle stood guard outside as the bursting drivers crowded inside...

What an immense job, but what incredible goodwill. It was a miracle. Nobody minded the waiting... The atmosphere sparkled as everyone worked determinedly together to ensure that this election would work.

And of course it did.

1999 AND ALL THAT

IT'S ALL RELOOTIVE

The wage differential between management and labour is the bane of unions – and nowhere more so than in South Africa with its historical discrepancies. As the gold price slid to new lows in mid-1999, Jonathan Rosenthal began a piece about the cost of production in *Business Report* on July 30 with this observation:

> Every time Bobby Godsell, the chief executive of the world's biggest gold producer, goes to the loo during office hours, he costs the company about R70 in lost productivity, a bit more than it would cost the company to employ a mineworker for the day.
>
> Now this of course assumes that, while in the loo, Bobby is not adding value to the company by thinking of a new way to talk up the gold price, cut costs or other such value-adding notion.
>
> In contrast, when a mineworker goes to the loo, he costs the company about 50c, even if he is thinking of a better way to drill the face or talk up the gold price, because in all likelihood no one in management would listen to him.
>
> Take this a step further and it turns out that the average underground mine produces about 5.3 ounces of gold a month for each employee on the payroll, including Bobby.
>
> So the opportunity cost to Anglogold of paying for Bobby's ablutions instead of hiring another mineworker is really about R8 000 a month in lost revenue, or about six times the mineworker's monthly wage...

One of the authors in front of an 'International Toilet' in Ventersdorp in the late 1980's.

A ROUND THE WORLD
IN 80 PULLS

CONFUCIUS SAY:

If the chain still swings, the seat's
still warm.

For an overview of what's potting on the world scene, put your seat in the upright position, fasten your seat belt, grab the handle and let's go...

JAPAN TAKES THE LEAD

Michael Fitzpatrick of the *Telegraph* made a telling point in an article about hi-tech toilets on 14 May 1998:

Say what you like about scientists, but their minds are rarely in the lavatory. Which is rather a shame, because our present toilet arrangements seem to be resolutely stuck in the Victorian age...

Given the taboos associated with our daily ablutions, it is perhaps not surprising that the lavatory hasn't been subject to the kind of hi-tech tinkering afforded other, less offensive, household fixtures such as the washing machine. Perhaps we have our priorities wrong. Is a whiter-than-white wash more important than a stainless rump? The Japanese don't think so.

In the land where 'beautiful' literally means 'clean' it seems only natural to the Japanese that technology should be harnessed to create a truly modern lavatorial experience. It started with an elementary warming of the toilet seat. Since that inspired creation, Japanese plumbing companies have been loading extra features on to their toilets...

In the late Eighties someone had a great idea: a toilet which could check on your health. A snippet in the *Financial Mail*'s Did You Hear column in June 1987 read:

> What is described as the world's first 'intelligent' lavatory, providing an instant electronic health check-up, is being developed by a group of Japanese companies. The system is know as 'intelligent toilet first-thing-in-the-morning'.
>
> Within five minutes of sitting on the seat, data on heartbeat, blood pressure and temperature comes up on a liquid crystal display. A big selling feature is a revolutionary system for collecting urine and analysing it instantly for sugar, protein, blood and urobilinogen.
>
> Manufacturers aren't saying exactly where the sensors are located, save that it should appeal to those who enjoy having more than their egos stroked first thing in the morning.

By 1989, a new feature was being planned. Sapa-Reuter reported in October:

> A spokesman for the company said the toilet not only tested blood pressure, pulse and urine, but also stored the data for up to 130 days. 'In future, the medical data can be sent to hospitals directly by telephone line,' he added.

Some years later (the cutting is undated), the *Sunday Times* announced:

> The high tech toilet has arrived. The Japanese have developed a toilet which costs $7 000 and which

will analyse one's urine and send one's doctors the results down a telephone.

In a country where a visit to the doctor can be very expensive, this form of medical check-up in lieu, or even in loo, of the doctor can be a very efficient health check.

In medieval times, examining urine was just about all the doctor had to offer before he announced what was wrong with the patient. So this new toilet is simply bringing an old body test up to date...

If you come across one of these loos, this is how to get the best use out of it. Visit the loo first thing in the morning and pass urine in the usual way. When the toilet is flushed, instead of going down the drain, the sample is carefully whisked away to electronic sensors. These give readouts of any blood sugar, infected cells and protein in the urine.

One can only congratulate the Japanese who can spend a penny and save hundreds of yen in doctors' bills.

Though many public toilets in Japan are still squat-type (see PUBLIC CONVENIENCES), hotels and new homes are now generally equipped with luxurious western-style lavatories. Johan Bornman reported in his What You See Is What I Think column in the Computing section of *The Star* on 11 June 1996:

A TOUCHPAD FOR YOUR TOUCHE, THANKS TO TECHNOLOGY

The subject of this week's focus is: IT and the Touche ... and this time we beat even the infamous You magazine to the scoop...

A company called Toto has decided that the time is ripe to introduce high technology to a lowly area of the anatomy – the humble but essential posterior.

At the touch of a button, Toto's new washlet called Zoe ... 'bathes your body with a soft, cleansing, aerated stream of water.' ... It also draws in odours, breaks down their molecules and leaves you with only clean air.

Best of all ... Zoe works with information technology borrowed from Sony or Nintendo. The red button controls the temperature, a smiley-curved volume button gives you more or less of that deliciously soft, aerated water and a touch-pad directs the stream right to where it is needed most...

I suggest you practise the art of touch-padding on a Nintendo before driving this machine. Just imagine the effect of carelessly fiddling with the red button instead of the blue or not quite getting the hang of the omni-directional spout or cranking up the volume too loudly or... Eina!

Michael Fitzpatrick enlarged on the Washlet in his 1998 *Telegraph* article:

This is a bidet-cum-lavatory that will wash you, dry you, even analyse your urine, take your blood pressure and then send the statistics to your doctor via a built-in modem...

Toto, which sells £245 million worth of high-tech Washlet toilets a year, makes the basic hi-tech Washlet for around £2 000. For this, your new toilet comes with an array of controls, including those for lifting the lid and seat automatically, activating a warm-water sprayer (which appears like a wand from beneath the rim), the dryer, and the toilet flush simulator. The latter is a requirement by genteel Japanese who like to disguise any tell-tale tinkle with the sound of a well-flushed loo before they get down to business. The simulator feature broadcasts the flush electronically, thereby saving blushes and precious water.

Then there is the portable bidet: 'not a laptop, more a lap-bottom':

> The half-pound Travel Washlet is a battery-powered contraption that can deliver a steady stream of up to 200cc of warm water to your undercarriage for up to 30 seconds. The device is filled with warm water before your departure to ablutions-hostile territory and will keep the priceless water warm until it is needed. The £60, hand-held unit runs on two AA batteries and has proved a winner with fastidious Americans and Japanese. Toto has sold more than 180 000 in the past two years.

Conquerors of the current macho challenge, Mt Kilimanjaro, would agree with John Button, who climbed it a few years ago:

> On the upper part of the mountain at 15 000 feet, toilet facilities consist of a row of doors behind each of which is what appears to be a fairly standard thunder box – until you lift the lid and see that you are about to sit over a hole in a piece of wood with a sheer drop of about 500ft beneath you. It is very cold and windy up there and there is no water at this altitude. A portable bidet would have been very useful. It would be especially nice if one could be sure the water was above freezing point.

In November 1998, a Sapa-AP dispatch gave travellers useful advice on how to use the latest Washlet model:

> It has got gadgets galore. But with its push-button control panel, whirring sprayers and automatic dryer,

a state-of-the-art Japanese toilet can be daunting. Here's a quick primer on the popular Washlet line:

Cleansing - The pressurised water sprayer features a telescoping nozzle to direct the cleansing stream of warm water. All models come with 'soft start', ie the spray begins at low pressure and increases in intensity. More advanced designs offer a pulsating massage spray.

Comfortable - Standard equipment includes a heated seat and a slam-proof lid. A built-in-the-bowl deodorising filter ... can be set to deodorise the air during or after use. Upscale models offer remote-control flushing and timers to control the seat temperature and other functions.

Hygienic - All Washlets come with a self-cleaning spray nozzle and an antibacterial coating on the seat. On the top-of-the-line model, the seat and cover are opened and closed by remote control so the user never has to touch unhygienic surfaces.

Expensive - Prices range from R3 640 for a bidet-equipped seat that fits on an existing toilet bowl to R21 280 for the ultimate model. A hand-held travel bidet goes for R532.

There are spanners in the waterworks, however. As we were putting this book together, a more alarming Sapa-AP report from Tokyo appeared in *The Star* of 7 July 1999:

HIGH-TECH TOILETS IN JAPAN UNDER FIRE

Firefighters are warning of blazes starting in high-tech toilets with heated seats which are so popular they are in a third of Japanese homes.

The special toilets blast a cleansing stream of water through a nozzle at the back, and then send out warm air for drying. But they can also start fires, especially when they grow old and aren't maintained properly, a Tokyo fire department official said yesterday.

At least three fires in the Tokyo area – in 1993, last year and April this year – have been blamed on the toilets. The toilet that caused the fire in April was made 18 years ago and had been leaking, said Yojiro Watanabe, spokesman for Tokyo-based toilet manufacturer Toto.

ALL MOD CONS

Hundreds of Shanghai women, including actresses, doctors and Communist Party officials, have replied to an advertisement for a wife placed by a man boasting an income of R3 000 a year and a flat with a toilet.

– *The Independent*, London, March 1988

NETHER AFFAIRS IN THE NETHERLANDS

Small, crowded Holland has similar problems to Japan. An upwardly mobile Dutch invention made it into *Time* magazine on 17 July 1995:

LOOK, NO HANDS

Fed up with people who thoughtlessly leave public toilets a splashy mess after flushing, Dutch interior designer Jurgen Erich and civil engineer Dirk Verhoog have devised a self-lifting toilet seat. Using pneumatic-driven springs, the seat slowly moves upright after use; it requires only a slight force to descend again. The Dutch partners hope to flush out some profits by marketing their product within a year.

Mass movements can be a problem too. On 21 June 1988, *The Star* ran a small paragraph on a potential crisis under the heading:

> ## DUTCH FEAR RUSH TO FLUSH
>
> AMSTERDAM. - Authorities in this dike-protected nation are taking water precautions during a soccer match on Tuesday.
>
> They fear the Dutch will all flush their toilets at the same time. Work will stop on a pipe project during live television coverage of the game between the Netherlands and West Germany. Brabant province fears mass, synchronised toilet-flushing would put pressure on the water system because 'a lot of people go to the toilet immediately after a televised match.'

Brabant is clearly a province in which people have to watch their step. David Walker wrote in Walker at Large in *The Star* of 20 July 1992:

> Holland. The name conjures up images of field upon field of colourful tulips. All very uplifting and romantic. But try tiptoeing through that lot and you're liable to find yourself really putting your foot in IT.
>
> The Netherlands, you see, as the world's third largest exporter of farm products, has nearly as many pigs as people and six times as many chickens, plus five million cows. The end result is an annual 80-million-ton manure mountain which amounts

to an enormous environmental problem – and in some areas, a pedestrian's nightmare.

Apart from the pong, run-off from the manure is polluting waterways while ammonia evaporates and causes acid rain, which in turn does nasty things to the soil. Farmers are given manure quotas which are rigidly enforced by stiff penalties on offenders. But there are still those who dump the stuff illicitly.

The problem is so serious that a special unit of inspectors, equipped with helicopters, has been set up in the province Noord Brabant – which contains a third of all Dutch pigs and hens – to hunt down the manure smugglers. They patrol by land and air, staging lightning raids and inspecting farmers' books and livestock numbers...

The English have dubbed the inspectors the Dung-ho Brigade.

ANOTHER SMUGGLERS' TALE

Sapa-AFP wired this item from Toronto in January 1995:

Canadian police and customs officials confirmed yesterday that they have spent about R50 000 to build two toilets without a flush.

The 'super loos' will be reserved for the exclusive use of travellers suspected of smuggling drugs in their bodies.

Suspects will be escorted to the flushless loos at Toronto's Pearson International Airport, and if necessary they will be provided with prune juice to help them flush out the necessary evidence.

Staff Sergeant Bill Matheson of the Royal Canadian Mounted Police drug squad said: 'It's mind-boggling when you think that some of the drugs that get past us and are now being used on the street came into Canada from up somebody's rear end.'

The new loos are metal toilet structures, each with a glass wall and a glass catch-chamber. Inspecting officers, wearing gloves, can spray down the faeces with water to see if it contains drug parcels.

By 1999 the Dutch problem had escalated despite the quotas. On 5 July, *Time* magazine reported in a lead story about factory farming:

Fifteen million pigs and 30 million laying hens, without counting all the other animals, produce more waste than the Netherlands' shallow soil cover can hope to absorb... UK farms alone produce more than 80 million tons of animal excreta a year.

Even in a relatively big country like France, waste contamination has reached drastic proportions in some parts. Brittany ... is an ecological nightmare. Two years ago, a third of Brittany's water supply had nitrate levels above the European legal maximum; in the next few years it is expected to rise to 80%. Seventy-one villages have been declared saturated by slurry.

SCALING THE HEIGHTS

David Walker's column in *The Star* had a fragrant sense of humour. In August 1990 one piece was headlined:

FINALLY, NO MORE UPS AND DOWNS

From the lofty heights of Cologne Cathedral comes a good-news story tailored to ease those Monday blues. At long last – 700 years, give or take a decade or two – a touch of what they regard as luxury has come the way of the artisans who look after the roof and towers of the Gothic building: a loo has been installed for them 70 m above the nave.

First to express thanks for this relief was Erwin Woyke, a master roofer who has worked in the cathedral for 37 years and who estimates that hundreds of working days have been wasted climbing up and down to the vestry lavatory.

He failed to mention what a pleasure it must be to flush your toilet with eau de Cologne.

News on an even higher plane came from Reuters in September 1994 (when the portable Travel Washlet was still to be invented):

THE ROOF OF THE WORLD TO GET EXPENSIVE LONG-DROP

GLASGOW. - British scientists preparing to climb Mount Everest yesterday were given their first glimpse of a toilet specially designed for use on the roof of the world.

The steel cubicle, equipped with steel guy ropes anchored with ice picks to stop it being blown off the mountain, has a wooden seat as plastic would be cold to the touch and crack in the freezing temperatures. A Scottish firm designed the R25 000 toilet that is to be taken by Sherpas up the mountain in seven pieces.

After its use by the 55-member British expedition, it will be dismantled and reassembled further down the mountain as a gift for other climbers caught short on the way up or down.

If ever there were a case for a really efficient seat-warmer...

THUNDER DOWN UNDER

Expense was no object for an Australian politician whose luxurious loo raised the ire of voters in Queensland earlier this year. A Sapa-DP report in February was headed:

AUSSIES DON'T LIKE THE CHEAP SEATS

SYDNEY. - Lavish spending on a minister's private toilet has embarrassed an Australian state government that came to power six months ago promising taxpayers to be careful with their money.

A toilet-roll holder worth A$97 and a waste bin with a price tag of A$255 ordered by Fair Trading Minister Judy Spence are at the heart of a scandal rocking the Queensland government.

Even the paint used in the redecoration was the best money could buy, opposition spokesperson Bruce Davidson said. 'Michelangelo could have done the job cheaper.'

BUCKING THE CISTERN

Australia was also the scene of a splash made by Prince Philip as a young man, according to the *Weekend Argus* in July 1992:

LONDON. - Prince Philip, Duke of Edinburgh, was once arrested for urinating on the pavement, says a new book published in Australia. The case of 'the Royal Wee' is revealed by author Bill Jenkings, whose work is being serialised in the Sydney *Sun Herald*.

Jenkings interviewed the Australian vice squad officer who came across the Prince in 1944, three years before his marriage to the Queen, doing what Aussies usually describe as 'pointing Percy at the pavement'.

The Prince was then a sailor on leave from the Royal Navy. His ship was docked near a notorious area called The Rocks. When he was asked his name he mumbled, according to the ex-policeman, a whole lot of 'wog' words. Philip's full name is Schleswig-Holstein-Sonderburg-Glucksburg.

By November 1989 he seems to have forgotten the joys of bucking the cistern. A *Sunday Times* reporter wrote from London:

Prince Philip went potty with rage when he smelt dagga in a loo at St James's Palace. 'Someone's been smoking bloody marijuana,' he bellowed at an aide during a reception for 200 teenagers.

A furious Philip has ordered the trustees of his award scheme to probe drug-taking among its entrants. The prince made his shock discovery when the youngsters – all 16 and over – collected gold awards at the palace. He went to wash his hands during a break in the reception – and caught a tell-tale whiff of the drug.

A royal insider revealed: 'He was still angry when he got back to Buckingham Palace. It obviously hit home more because it went on right underneath his nose. His fury was such that one aide had to warn the organisers of an event he was attending that evening of his brittle mood.'

Gone to pot, that St James's Palace.

BRITISH SENSIBILITIES

Joe Bromilow, the marketing manager for Andrex (British toilet paper manufacturers) is reported by Michael Fitzpatrick as having said:

> The British are, undoubtedly, more delicately reared than their foreign counterparts. We are very sacrosanct about our lavatorial arrangements and we don't like to change them... Look at the bidet – it has never really captured our imagination and most of us are more likely to use it to wash our socks than our bottoms.

To sit or not to sit must be the dilemma of all eminent people asked to declare toilets open. Another James was invited to christen some cisterns in early February 1991, according to a *Star* report from London:

TORY MP GETS FIRST FLUSH

Tory MP Sir James Spicer has accepted an invitation to officially open a R75 000 toilet ... in Dorset's Piddle Valley. The toilet was installed at the first school in the valley, Piddletrentride, near Dorchester. Two years ago Sir James took the then Under Secretary of State for Education, John Butcher, to the school to see the antiquated lavatories for himself. Now he says: 'I've no doubt I'll be asked to sit on it, but I shall simply make a short speech and pour a bottle of water into the cistern just to ensure that it flushes properly.'

> ### NEWS FLASH!
>
> Britain now harbours fearsome plastic creatures called Bog Monsters, created by toy designer Simon Fearnehough, that lurk in the toilet and pop out when you raise the seat. The mind (need we say it?) boggles.

THE STARS AND PIPES FOREVER

The problem of finding the toilet in a dark bathroom seems to exercise American minds mightily. In July 1992, Sapa-AP reported a 10-year-old's prize-winning bright idea:

> LAKE MILLS (Wisconsin) - One of those useful ideas that no one ever thought of before – a glow-in-the-dark toilet seat – has earned Clint Lenz a place in the Smithsonian Institution. He said his seat eliminates the need for a night light and prevents fumbling in the dark to find the toilet.
>
> The idea came naturally to him: his father and some of his mother's relatives are plumbers... His father Fred got him a toilet seat and he covered it with glow-in-the-dark spray paint. It took first place in the 'household' division of the national Invent America competition. Clint and his parents will fly to Washington later this month... Mrs Lenz said relatives and friends are lining up for the illuminating latrines and his grandfather is encouraging him to apply for a patent.

Then the *New Scientist* got in on the act. Its Feedback column of 2 April 1994 opened dramatically with the following scenario:

> It is night. Consequently, it is dark. In the small hours ... you make your way to the bathroom and head for where you hope the toilet is ... and then sit down. The toilet seat feels dank and cold and you no longer fit onto it properly. This is because it isn't there. Someone ... left it up before going to bed and you are sitting on the top of the toilet bowl. 'Yeughk!'
>
> The piece goes on to describe a solution for those venturing into dark bathrooms for relief: the Watercolor Intelligent Nightlight (WIN) which will tell you whether the toilet seat is up or down with the help of a photocell and a motion detector. Its inventor, Bryan Patrie, explains:
>
> When it detects your presence ... WIN, which is attached to the bottom of the seat, shines an infrared beam upwards and if the beam is reflected back, the seat must be up. Then it will give a red signal, warning women, in particular. If the seat is down, a green light, or 'all systems go' ... comes on... It (also) shines down into the bowl and provides men with what might be called 'visual targeting guidance'.

The punchline that comes at the end applies to both inventions:

> Feedback, who salutes Patrie's ingenuity but has never had the difficulty his invention aims to resolve, is puzzled about one small thing. Why doesn't everyone just switch on the bathroom light?

> ## BUM RAP
>
> The latest edition of the police magazine Servamus reports that an American coach driver radioed police when an old lady said there was a bomb in the loo. As passengers poured out and bomb experts moved in to look for the device, the old dear said: 'I said there was a bum in the toilet.' A hobo was indeed found there and flushed out.
>
> – *The Star*, 9 June 1991

OUT OF THIS WORLD

One of the questions most often asked of astronauts features in this report from Hugh Roberton of *The Star*'s Foreign News Service on 9 January 1993:

WASHINGTON: - How do astronauts go to the toilet? The answer is complicated and is the centre of a R90 million argument after an inquiry revealed that the costs of designing and making a toilet for use by both men and women had shot up by some 900%. It will cost $6 million, excluding research, to build a flight-certified production model.

In early space flights, male astronauts wore urination bags and no provision was made for defecation. They ate low-residue meals before a launch. Journeys rarely exceeded 36 hours, and it worked. But longer trips and women astronauts called for a rethink.

The Soviet solution – liquids separated into oxygen and hydrogen and the oxygen recirculated with solids kept in bags – was considered inefficient.

The US system, described as the most advanced toilet conceived, is an elaborate contraption in which high-pressure jets of very cold air under the seat carry the waste into a tank.

Within a week, the cost of experimental astro-toilets seems to have escalated outasight. Sapa-AP reported on 16 January, also in *The Star*:

ASTRONAUTS FORGOT CHAIN REACTION
HOUSTON (Texas) - Even when the toilet costs $23 million, some folks can't seem to remember to put the lid down. The crew of four men and one woman aboard space shuttle *Endeavour* got a scolding when Mission Control on Thursday noticed that a fan on the experimental new toilet was still running – meaning the lid was still up.

Mission Control's Carl Meade had astronaut Gregory Harbaugh take care of the problem: 'And Endeavour, in the future, we would like you to make sure that lid is closed and that fan cycles off, if you could remember.'

'Okay, Carl,' Harbaugh said. 'That's a good reminder.' There was no word from Nasa on which astronaut was the offender.

Endeavour's astronauts are the first to test the new toilet. It can accommodate much more waste than the old model – essential if shuttle flights are to exceed two weeks – but has been condemned as too pricey.

On the first manned trip to Mars, we recommend giant rubber bands.

TRAVEL TIP:

Parisians have dedicated a museum to their extensive sewerage system, through which three million baguettes, 1 000 tons of fruit and 100 tons of fish pass every day. Visitors to the museum are even afforded a tour of some working tunnels, located on the river bank at Quai d'Orsay.

– From *Bush Telegraph* in the *Daily Telegraph*, 26 July 1997

DECKING THE WALLS

In September 1984 the *Sunday Times* reported:

> Britons spend an average of four months in a normal lifetime in the loo, a new survey has revealed. For many people it has become a place of refuge where they can read, meditate … or simply escape from other members of the family.

Sadly for those who seek refuge, the decline of the grand lavatory continues. Most toilets today are cramped, dark and boring by comparison, which must add to the sum of human woes.

In the home, they tend to be gloomy vertical boxes on the south side where, as the phrase goes, the sun don't shine. Small wonder that ever more people suffer from piles and constipation and that scourge of the neurotic kugel and over-achieving yuppy, the spastic colon. (Tim always complains of his spastic semi-colons).

Public toilets are even worse, with their rows of flimsy-walled stalls that offer scant privacy. And to our collective shame, township and squatter camp toilets remain – to coin a phrase – the pits.

Second in importance only to a snug, weatherproof roof over one's head must be the right to a decent and private privy. Our Water Affairs Ministry's laudable intention to provide running water to everyone in time should surely be extrapolated to include, if not waterborne sanitation, at least a VIP toilet (see THE SERIOUS SECTION) for every household. Kleinhuisies before corvettes, ek sê.

CLOSET OBSERVATIONS

Toilet decor in general leaves a lot to be desired. Richard Gordon (of *Doctor in the House* fame) wrote a treatise on modern living called *Good Neighbours : Suburbia Observed* which makes some telling points:

> The bathroom, which may nor may not have a sep. W.C., is a singularly anomalous place in the abode. It is the site of the family's most intimate activities, yet it must be freely open on Sunday mornings as part of the display activity. Failure to offer this unstinted hospitality may incite hostile tribal suspicion...
>
> This paradox – a secret apartment periodically thrown open to the public – demands a high standard of sanitation...
>
> In the sep. W.C., Airwick is permissible, and devices which colour the water like squirts from a squid are passable. But not porcelain plaques with jokes, or Here's the Wee Room amid forget- me-nots on the door. Musical toilet rolls are out, and musical seats definitely so.

Jilly Cooper's famous book on *Class* (great lavatory reading) has a section on the bathroom decor of those with social pretensions.

THE UPPER-CLASS BATHROOM
The bath and basin are always white; the lavatory is white with a chain that pulls and a wooden seat which is often agonisingly cracked, and gives exquisite pain by nipping the Old School bottom. All upper class loos smell of asparagus pee in June...

THE MIDDLE-CLASS BATHROOM
Since the middle classes discovered sex in the seventies, (Samantha would) probably have a bidet in the bathroom... In the downstairs lavatory, as a sort of 'bogography', Gideon modestly records his

achievements, with photographs of himself in school hockey, rugger and cricket teams.

THE NOUVEAU RICHE LAV

In every room musak pours out of speakers, even in the loos, which have musical lavatory paper, fur carpets and chandeliers.

Mr Nouveau-Richards responded to an ad in *House & Garden*: 'After years of mass-produced plastic, feel the warmth of solid mahogany ... and we offer as an option at no extra cost a brass plaque recessed into the lid for your personal inscription.' Mr Nouveau-Richards has 'Piss Off' wittily inscribed on his.

THE LOWER-MIDDLE-CLASS BATHROOM

The matching bathroom suite, in sky blue or avocado, with a basin shaped like a champagne glass, has a matching toilet cover, toilet surround and bathmat in washable sky-blue nylon fur. A Spanish 'dolly' with Carmen skirts discreetly conceals the toilet tissue... Jen (Teale), being obsessed by unpleasant odours, has Airwick, potpourri and a pomander on top of the cistern, and a deodorant block hanging like a sloth inside. In the toilet there is bright blue water.

THE WORKING-CLASS LAV

Working class houses and flats tend to smell of cabbage and leaky gas... The Bronco is hung up with string in the outside lavatory, which is probably shared with several other families. This explains why so many of the working classes suffer from constipation.

And here is our own Maureen Isaacson in *Smooching Beryl*:

I wouldn't say my mom's taste was on overload either. Not if you see the way she's done out our house – china dolls and lots of pink. Even that grim fluffy stuff on the toilet seats is pink.

She's only into the toilet hey. *Reader's Digest* and *Huisgenoot* lined up on the cochineal book stand, same colour as the toilet roll holder, *Desiderata* on the door, framed, mind you. All about going placidly in the noise and haste. I tell you the only place you could go placidly in that household was the flipping 'loo', as Mom used to call it.

GREENS PLEASE NOTE ...

The winds of change are even blowing through lavatories now. Sue Townsend's immortal Adrian Mole takes a job in *True Confessions of Adrian Albert Mole* and finds himself in deep trouble with his boss, Mr Brown, an eco-freak:

He turned and glowered at me. 'I have just heard a disquieting fact about you, Mole,' he said.

'Oh,' I said.

'Oh, indeed,' repeated Brown. 'Is there something you should tell me about your lavatorial habits, Mole?'

After a period of thought I said, 'No sir, if it's about the puddle on the floor last Friday, that was when I...'

'No, no, not at work, at home,' he snapped. I thought about the lavatory at home. Surely I used it as other men did? Or did I? Was I doing something unspeakable without knowing it? And if I was how did Brown know?

'Think of your lavatory seat, Mole. You have been heard bragging about it, in the canteen.' As I was bidden I thought about the newly installed lavatory seat at home.

'Describe the aforementioned lavatory seat, Mole.'

I fingered my penknife nervously. Brown had obviously gone mad... 'Well sir,' I said, edging imperceptibly towards the door. 'It's sort of a reddish brown wood, and it has brass fittings...'

Brown shouted, 'Ha, reddish brown wood! ... Mahogany! You are a vandal, Mole, an enemy of the earth. Consider your job to be on the line! Mahogany is one of the earth's most precious and endangered woods and you have further endangered it by your vanity and lust.'

THE SALUBRIOUS LOO

Now to practicalities. Toilet decor in South Africa is sadly neglected – and we're not talking striped wallpaper and chandeliers, but a positive striving for a more salubrious atmosphere. But there is much that can be done to redeem even the meanest sanctum of sanitation. These littlest rooms cost so little to renovate that even the wildest flights of fantasy, if they fail, can be painted over at minimum expense and effort.

The best instant solution either of us has seen for a family lav had fibre-board nailed on the walls and operated as a floor-to-ceiling notice board covered with posters, prints, cartoons, photos, maps, cuttings, a calendar and kids' paintings (a never-ending procession when they're at nursery school). Everyone in the family contributed, adding things they found interesting or controversial, so there were always new items to study.

Most lavs would take happily to this treatment. If the walls are smooth enough, all you need is sticky tape and Presstick. If you're worried about the walls getting acne, put up a notice board and keep it well supplied with thumb tacks. The thoughtful host will also add a tear-off notepad with attached pencil for doodling and graffiti or jotting down significant thoughts.

There is no reason why the larger loo should not serve in a dual-purpose capacity either. Cloakrooms are old hat, but if you have the space, try following the example of the Cockrams' south-facing lavatory-cum-wine cellar in Johannesburg where the temperature is cool and constant and the contemplation of labels evokes anticipatory pleasure.

Despite Jilly Cooper's caustic comment about 'bogography', we think the lav is also a good place to display old photographs, specially of the sports teams you once played in which are solid proof to doubters that you once had hair and a waistline.

Framed cartoons are favoured by some – even the high and mighty. In January 1984 *Sunday Times* cartoonist Dave Gaskill scored a major coup with a Thatcher cartoon. His journalist colleague Gwen Gill (now the gimlet-eyed chronicler of South African society and scourge of the pretentious) wrote:

> It was the event of the week – the day the blushing Cartoonist met the reluctant Consort and helped to furnish the loo at Number 10 Downing Street.
>
> They don't come much coyer than Denis Thatcher where the Press is concerned. So it was great power to the drawing pen of cartoonist Dave Gaskill when he chatted with Mrs Thatcher's other half and handed over a *Sunday Times* cartoon that had 'tickled Denis pink'.
>
> The Burmah Oil Company, one of Mr T's hosts during his South African trip, had earlier asked Mr Gaskill if they could have the cartoon as a memento

for their visitor – and requested he should have it framed and make the presentation personally.

At the unique handover, the British Prime Minister's husband told Dave he had just the right spot for it – in the Number 10 lav!

From a 1996 news item:

Princess Diana has decorated her lavatory at Kensington Palace with 12 framed cartoons of Camilla Parker Bowles. 'All the best cartoons from the national newspapers about Charles and Camilla are down there,' a recent visitor said.

OTHER APPURTENANCES

These should be carefully chosen since they are on public display and reflect your taste and style. A removable shelf fixed from wall to wall across the top of the cistern is a good height and makes a handy repository (it needs to be removable so you can get at the cistern).

Essentials: suitable literature (see following chapter); a copy of *Pees & Queues;* good soap; a clean hand towel; an inconspicuous but visible extra bogroll; a concealed brush for emergencies.

Consider: a box of tissues; hand lotion; extra laundered and folded hand towels; a pad and pencil for sudden inspirations; an ashtray only if there are smokers.

No-nos: tsatskes; all forms of macramé and crochet work; 3-piece fun fur toilet sets; plastic things that hang on the bowl rim and turn the water a virulent blue; pot plants (they die); all substances that purport to banish pongs (they don't).

SO GET WITH IT...

This is your chance to lash out with paint, glue and nails. Having lost our chains and thrones, the very least we deserve is a salubrious loo.

PAINTING IN THE CAN

No wonder composer Andrew Lloyd Webber looked somewhat startled on Monday night when he appeared before the TV cameras for the first time with his £10 million Canaletto painting, *The Old Horse Guards*. His art dealer David Mason had just told him that the initial cleaning of the 18th century masterpiece had uncovered a lavatorial joke by Canaletto – in a corner of the canvas are two small men shown relieving themselves against a wall.

'I was staggered, but David was right. It's in there,' Lloyd Webber said afterwards. 'I must be the first bloke to pay £10 million for a painting of two blokes piddling against a wall.'

The painting is to be hung in the Tate Gallery, where no doubt it will bring a bit of light relief.

– From Thomas Cobbleigh, *Sunday Times* May 3 1992

READING MATTER

First some statistics. According to *The Toilet Book*, the average healthy person spends 11½ minutes a day in the lavatory, which amounts to a little over 1 hour 20 minutes a week, well over a quarter of a day a month and nearly half a week every year. So the daily stint, added up, gives you plenty of time to feast your eyes and broaden your mind if the surroundings are pleasant.

STOCKING THE BOOKSHELF

The main criteria for reading matter in a family lav are: a broad variety and a regular turnover of items that the sitter can dip into without becoming so engrossed that a queue forms outside the door. Magazines and illustrated wildlife books are good for a quick read; so is the newspaper. If your privy is exclusive, however, you may like to emulate the Vereeniging businessman who managed to get through the complete works of Shakespeare in three years and has now started on Chaucer.

Humour goes down well in lavs, as do books in the useless information category such as *The Guinness Book of Records;* the thunderbox is the ideal place for secretly boning up on Trivial Pursuit questions. Further suggestions include: any edition of *Madam & Eve, A Dictionary of South African English, Brewer's Dictionary of Phrase & Fable, The Book of Insults* (learn picturesque new phrases While-U-Sit), *The Whole Earth Catalog, Class* by Jilly Cooper, Arthur Goldstuck's urban legends and collections of short pieces by Peter Ustinov, Erma Bombeck, Gus Silber or Alan Coren.

Serious-minded sitters go for more edifying works like dictionaries, almanacs and collections of quotations and poetry. Novels are an absolute no-no in busy households – though Henry Miller disagrees:

All my good reading, you might say, was done in the toilet... There are passages of *Ulysses* which can be read only in the toilet – if one wants to extract the full flavour of their content.

Lord Chesterfield, in his Letters to his Son, 1747:

I knew a gentleman who was so good a manager of his time that he would not even lose that small portion of it which the call of nature obliged him to pass in the necessary-house; but gradually went through all the Latin poets, in those moments. He bought, for example, a common edition of Horace, of which he tore off gradually a couple of pages, carried them with him to that necessary place, read them first and then sent them down as a sacrifice to Cloacina; thus was much time fairly gained; and I recommend you to follow his example. It is better than only doing what you cannot help doing at those moments and it will make any book which you shall read in that manner, very present in your mind.

LOOTERARY INSULTS

Writers from Alexander Pope onwards have used the privy as a symbol of extreme insult. James Dickey, the American poet and writer of that extraordinary novel about the darker side of male bonding, *Deliverance*, said of a fellow poet:

If it were thought that anything I wrote was influenced by Robert Frost, I would take that particular work of mine, shred it, and flush it down the toilet, hoping not to clog the pipes. A more sententious, holding-forth old bore who expected every hero-worshipping adenoidal little twerp of a student-poet to hang on his every word I never saw.

Quentin Crisp wrote of Oscar Wilde:

> He festooned the dung heap on which he had placed himself with sonnets as people grow honeysuckle around outdoor privies.

And Arthur Calder-Marshall sneered:

> The bestseller ... gives an idea of what is read on the periphery of literacy, the reading matter of those who have graduated from the literature of the lavatory wall to the printed word.

A MORE CREATIVE ACTIVITY

Writers, being given to introspection, do a lot of thinking on the loo – Martin Luther (in the play at least) being a prime example. And one stand-up comic takes it even further. John Beck reported from New York in March 1999:

> At 69, Bob Newhart is finally revealing one of his coveted trade secrets to stand-up comedy – call it an ode to the power of porcelain.
>
> 'The best routines I ever wrote, I wrote in a john, I think,' he says in his usual deadpan delivery. 'There should be a book on it, but I think if someone

researched it, most of the great ideas since the beginning of time probably came out in the john.'

Of all places, why the bathroom?

'Because there is nothing to distract you. If you've been in one john, you've been in all the johns in the world. So your mind is kind of focused.'

Taken in context with the past 40 years of his career, this may be one of the dirtiest jokes that the comedian has ever told in public. Bob Newhart, the buttoned-down, guy-next-door icon of American comedy, using toilet humour?

WARNING !!

Don't overdo the private mind-improvement or literary sessions, however. *The Independent* News Service warned on 23 January 1989:

LOO READING MAY BE BAD FOR YOU

Reading in the loo is bad for you: if you are constipated, it may give you piles. This is just one observation made by doctors at the Department of Surgery, John Radcliffe Hospital, Oxford, who compared the habits of 100 people with haemorrhoids, with 100 unaffected people. They report in the British medical journal, *The Lancet*, that reading per se is not bad for you, but sitting on the toilet for long periods relaxes the sphincter muscles round the anus. This, coupled with repeated straining, may create the ideal conditions for developing haemorrhoids.

GRAFFITI

If you find for your verse there's no call
And you can't afford paper at all
For the poet true born
However forlorn
There's always the lavatory wall.

In public toilets where the obscene is the norm, witty graffiti are a rare and declining art form; it takes genius to coin a gem like 'Prune juice shall set you free'. There are also people who've made a career of collecting graffiti and enshrining them in books which make fine and funny lav reading, so we're giving you a few pages on which to compose your own graffiti – and simply passing on a heartfelt lament.

Media man Chris Moerdyk, whose perceptive and entertaining TV programmes featuring advertising from all over the world are a weekly must-watch, has written for the Independent Group for some years. In one of his Whispers columns in September 1997 he wrote:

I am at a loss to understand why it is that while most media stride forward with brave innovation, the oldest and often the most entertaining medium of our times has become boring to the extreme. When it exists at all.

There was a time when one could escape from everything by reading the most creative of litanies behind the lavatory door. Heaven knows what has happened. An outbreak of compulsive cleaning disorders among public toilet supervisors? Or is all that creative genius being channelled into the Internet?

It is sorely missed.

ULTIMATE ACCOLADE

It passed the cold bum test.

Actor Bob Hoskins about a riveting film script that kept him sitting on the loo too long.

And a closing ditty by Alan Bennett, from the Faber *Book of Parodies*:

Here I sit, alone and sixty,
Bald and fat, and full of sin,
Cold the seat and loud the cistern
As I read the Harpic tin.

The littlest room doesn't have to be that way, however. As *The Toilet Book* says:

It is possible to concentrate and learn only when one is feeling relaxed and confident. In the privacy and comfort of your own toilet, in your own home, conditions should be ideal... The toilet should be a temple of knowledge, not of fear.

GRAFFITI PAGE

In case of emergency, tear here.

GRAFFITI PAGE

In case of emergency, tear here.

THE SERIOUS
SECTION

Let's get serious now. A 1997 United Nations report warned that half the world's people don't have access to a toilet or even a decent latrine – a number that grew from 2.6 billion in 1990 to 2.9 billion in that year, and is probably over 3 billion today. The lack of adequate toilets in rural areas (where only 18% of people have access) and the grossly insanitary conditions in slum areas and shanty towns that burgeon daily as people crowd into the cities increase the likelihood of epidemics. Cholera, typhoid, bilharzia, gastroenteritis and other illnesses kill 2.2 million children each year.

The article in the *Argus* in July 1997 that gave the above figures went on to quote three officials involved in environmental health:

'The international community often focuses on one vogue issue when the basic things are often the greatest killers,' said Joe Crownover, director of a field programme in Latin America...

'Sanitation is not a sexy issue,' said Dennis Warner, chief of rural environmental health at the World Health Organisation...

'The funds are available. The question is the government's priorities,' said Jos Hueb, a sanitation engineer.

And the startling figure quoted to correct this situation?

The UN Children's Fund (Unicef) said the problem could be solved in 10 years by spending an amount equal to about 10% of global military expenditures for one year.

We would go further than the WHO and suggest that since the people who hold the world's purse-strings are 100% blessed with waterborne sanitation, there is no real incentive to address the problems of those whose lives are blighted by its absence.

Waterborne sanitation is one of humankind's greatest inventions – when it is properly installed and maintained. But millions of people find themselves on the receiving end of a waterborne system with no treatment works, a common occurrence in the developing world, or a system that fails with raw sewage spewing out all over the place. Waterborne sewage is characterised by flush and forget. When the user flushes the toilet, the problem goes away and it is up to someone else to solve it. Even if they don't, you don't care because it is downstream from you – that is, until someone upstream discharges their sewage on to you!

The 'sexy issue' that generated extraordinary publicity in the South African media (and the most vociferous protest from the public) over the past year was the ill-treatment of what experts call 'charismatic animals': the baby elephants. Children dying in their millions because of poor sanitation don't make nearly such good copy. Shame on us.

THE VIP TOILET

But there is a small light shining in the African outhouse: the Blair or Ventilated Improved Pit toilet. This sanitary innovation was first developed by a British-trained marine biologist called Dr Peter Morgan who joined Zimbabwe's Blair Research Laboratory in 1972 to study the spread of waterborne diseases due to poor sanitation. The *Sunday Times* reported in October 1991:

> He designed an earth toilet that is fly and odour free and does not need a water supply ...a design which has spread throughout the Third World

without a cent in patent royalties going back to Dr Morgan or the Zimbabwean government.

'We wanted the knowledge to be freely available to anybody throughout the world,' says the man who has probably saved countless Third World people from such diseases as cholera, typhoid, dysentery, bilharzia and diarrhoea.

When the Queen visited Zimbabwe that year, she awarded him the OBE.

David Robbins highlighted Dr Morgan and his Blair toilet in a Health Africa article in *The Star*, April 21 1994:

His job was to design a safe and cost-effective toilet which could be mass-produced. The result was the Blair, a variation of the pit latrine which incorporates a chimney or vent to reduce odours and trap flies. Morgan's basic design has found its way into large sections of the Third World, including South Africa.

The design is based on air-flow: the latrine is built in a spiral or U shape with a door-less entrance facing the prevailing wind and an open squat-hole over a pit ventilated by a pipe or brick shaft. This creates a flow of clean air in through the doorway, down the hole, across the surface of the pit contents and up through the ventilator shaft, which has a strong up-draught because it rises above the latrine roof.

The Blair design has many advantages. It is relatively cheap compared with standard brick toilets and can be built by people with basic bricklaying skills. The spiral or U-shape gives privacy to latrine users without the expense of a door. The direction of the air flow draws odours away from the toilet and the pit up the vent pipe, to disperse high in the air. Flies that get into the latrine gravitate towards the light at the top of the vent pipe which is covered with fly screening that traps them (so they fall to their death in the pit) and keeps out any flies attracted by the smell. Where possible, the concrete floor is plastered so that it slopes towards the squat-hole, making the latrine easy to keep clean.

EYE SAY...

Researchers involved with one of the NGOs supplying VIP toilets have found that painting an eye on the toilet wall overlooking the squat-hole serves two purposes: feeling observed, toilet-users don't throw rubbish (like bottles and tins) down the hole that could interfere with the decomposition process – and they don't linger, either.

Thanks to concerted effort by the Zimbabwe Ministry of Health and the British-funded Mvuramanzi Trust, which works on water and sanitation initiatives in rural areas, an estimated 500 000 of these latrines have been built in rural areas, bringing decent sanitation to millions. The toilets are not given away: the Trust subsidises the cement and reinforcing mesh while the community must provide the bricks, sand and any other materials, as well as the labour. Education is also important:

> Dr Morgan says, 'It's not much of an improvement making use of a Blair toilet and then preparing food or eating it without first washing one's hands.'
> ...He's fitted tanks with a simple stopper for control, and is now conducting tests on how they are being used, or why they are not being used. He's even provided some toilets with a tray on the roof so water for an afternoon shower can be heated by the sun.

'Technically, anything's possible,' he says. 'The ultimate answer with regard to disease reduction lies in behaviour change which takes advantage of the new facilities.'

Education in third-world technology goes even further in Zimbabwe schools: pupils who take O-level general science are required to understand the principles of both Blair toilets and bush water pumps – and to build their own models.

For anyone interested in the detailed mechanics of the Blair toilet: the Department of Community Medicine at the University of Zimbabwe, in collaboration with the Ministry of Health, has developed a Builder's Instruction Manual for a double compartment latrine – one side for men, the other for women – which is available on the Internet at:

http://www.mediazw.com/blair/index.htm

HOW ARE WE DOING DOWN SOUTH?

We are approaching our sanitation problems from a different angle. Lacking the funds and natural resources (wood and clay for bricks) that were available in Zimbabwe, we are concentrating on improving existing pit toilets by adding ventilation and spreading the word about its advantages. The job is being handled by the Mvula Trust which has a mandate from the Department of Water Affairs & Forestry to run a programme that addresses the basic sanitation issues in rural areas: clean water, refuse removal and the containment of household waste.

Before we go into details, here is the sorry historical background.

During the apartheid years when people were being forced out of towns to desolate 'settlement areas' on bare veld and in the distant homelands, the Nationalist government tried to demonstrate its benevolent intentions by preparing the way with sanitation. In repeated shows of misdirected largesse, rows of corrugated iron kleinhuisies were erected to await the deportees. Bureaucracy being what it is, kleinhuisies mushroomed in many a ver verlate vlakte where they remained unused until they rotted, while those who really needed them crowded closer and closer in their shacks.

Where sanitation was officially provided, pit and bucket latrines, aquaprivies, etc, prevailed. As late as 5 February 1994, Julienne du Toit was writing in her environmental On Track column in the *Saturday Star*:

> South Africa still has to be toilet-trained. Where else in the world are there unused toilets as far as the eye can see in the middle of the veld, yet sewage is spilling out everywhere else?
>
> Whites are mostly well catered for, but the rest of the population struggle against a mentality that has moved no further than the old thunder pot under the bed...
>
> Last week (in Grahamstown), the rain came down in buckets. And in the two-year-old township of Rini, raw sewage began washing in great smelly clots down the streets. According to South Africa's oldest newspaper, *Grocott's Mail*, up to 200 pit latrines spilt their noisome contents after water seeped into the pits. The reason? The Urban Foundation's housing branch, funded in part by the Independent Development

Trust, had seen fit to build the pit latrines on a solid bed of clay.

(Interestingly, Richard Holden of the Mvula Trust – see next section – says that this shouldn't have been a problem. It was more likely that surface water was channelled into the pits which then overflowed. Another problem could be the disposal of washwater in built-up areas: if no facilities are provided, people tend to get rid of the water down the pit.)

Less than two months later, Julienne was reporting a similar mishap:

In a new township development called Poortje out near Ennerdale, the pit latrines are overflowing. (They were, in fact, aquaprivies which need emptying on a regular basis).

Residents claim that the Transvaal Provincial Administration has reneged on a deal to drain the toilets once a month. The last time the toilets were cleaned out was in the middle of last year ... and even then that was with a bakkie, and men emptying the slop with buckets. The raw sewage was then emptied into a field nearby, where children play.

Several people have dug pits adjoining the latrines to help drain the sewage and prevent it flowing into their yards. At one house, the worst possible scenario happened and a little girl fell into the open pit. Her father saved her, but said he still has nightmares about ducking his head under the disgusting mess, trying to find his daughter...

The problem is not a unique one. The same sort of scenario – the overflowing toilets and sewage systems and the angry residents – is happening all over the country.

Yet the VIP toilet had already arrived in certain areas, mainly because they were being pushed by sanitation experts who realised their value to cash-strapped councils. In 1992 Prof Gerrit Marais, before retiring as Professor of Water Resources and Public Health Engineering at UCT, gave an unusual speech at a graduation ceremony, reported by Sam Sole in the December 13 *Sunday Tribune:*

> A University of Cape Town professor surprised a graduation ceremony this week by talking crap for half an hour – literally...
>
> His message was simple... The provision of water and sanitation was more important than the provision of houses... People are nearly always able to provide themselves with some sort of shelter whereas the provision of appropriate sewerage systems was not within the individual's grasp... One of the biggest problems, he notes, is the provision of sanitation systems appropriate to the resources and education of the community.
>
> Prof Marais gave examples of two different approaches: a mediocre water-borne sewerage system at Mdantsane near East London, which kept getting blocked with rubbish like stones, newspaper and even pantihose because people were not used to flush sanitation, and the installation of VIP toilets at Bester's Camp outside Durban.
>
> Here the community was persuaded of the unaffordability and impracticality of a first-world system in the dense settlement of informal housing and opted for what is known as the VIP latrine. This variation on the basic deep hole in the ground has successfully addressed two of its main problems: odour and flies. The technology required for its construction is simple, it's cheap, and can be understood by the community.

He intended to keep busy 'mucking about with muck,' he concluded, because there was still much work to be done. He called the bucket system a 'sanitary horror story'.

ENTER THE MVULA TRUST

Richard Holden, the Technical Manager, explained its focus. Since funds are limited in South Africa, communities have decided to concentrate on improving existing long-drops by simply adding ventilation.

All that is needed is a 110mm PVC pipe sticking into the pit, clear of the sides, and extending 30cm above the roof of the toilet. The top of the pipe must be covered with wire mesh to trap any flies rising out of the pit. The resultant air flow through the squat hole and up the pipe instantly cuts down on both odour and flies.

One of the obvious problems with a Blair toilet is that when the pit fills up, a new structure has to be built. A better option for the truly poor is a wattle-and-daub structure with a good deep ventilated pit. If properly supported and well treated, a pit can last 20 years; in parts of North Africa they dig them 10 metres deep, to last a family several generations!

An alternative structure for those who can afford it is a galvanised iron kleinhuisie, complete with lockable door and lidded white plastic toilet. They're available from South African building supply merchants for around R400 and are prized by people who have never had decent sanitation. Again, the pit must be ventilated and the design of the pedestal is important, because it mustn't foul easily. The toilet lid doesn't need to be left open to create an air flow since there is a built-in gap under the seat.

So we're getting there, slowly. Better education will accelerate the process; one wonders if our high school science courses will ever require students to learn the principles of ventilated pit toilets and build their own models.

As we have said in a previous chapter, we believe in kleinhuisies before corvettes. Decent sanitation is a right, not a privilege.

COMPOSTING TOILETS

Composting toilets are the IN thing with the environmentally conscious – as are solar heaters, solar power cells, wind-generated electricity and natural or ecological houses – but the technology is still too expensive for the poor in South Africa.

TOILETS AND AIDS

Back in 1987 we weren't as savvy – and officialdom not nearly as worried – about AIDS as we are now, and there were a lot of misconceptions about how it is caught. In a reassuring article in the *Sunday Times* of June 7 of that year, Cas St Leger reported:

> More than half the people in South Africa believe you can catch AIDS from a lavatory seat – even though experts say you can't.
>
> A pilot survey had been conducted by IMS South Africa, Cas wrote, and among public misconceptions of how AIDS might be transmitted were:
>
> 65.5% believe it might be passed on by mosquitoes
>
> 64% by kissing

- 60% by taking a spa-bath with an AIDS sufferer (and 57.5% the day after), 44% taking a sauna and 43% using a swimming pool
- 53% believe it might be caught from a toilet seat
- 40% by sleeping in the same hotel bed the night after it was occupied by an AIDS carrier
- 13.5% by holding hands

The good news is that all these activities are quite safe – only sexual contact and the exchange of body fluids with an AIDS sufferer will transmit the virus.

Kleinhuisie: Privy: usu. an outdoor earth or bucket closet, occ. loosely, any lavatory. See also *P.K.* and *long-drop* cf. *Austral. dunny, dyke, shouse.* (*Afk. Klein* small + *huis* house + *dimin. suffix* -ie)

The N9 may be the smiling Gateway to Cape Town; the main line is surely ... the back door, past the dustbin and the kleinhuisie. *Cape Times* 28.2.72

First to go were the cluster of uithuisies, kleinhuisies, groothuisies and the tacked-on corrugated iron stoep. *Ibid* 16.8.73

It isn't only the weather and fire ... sometimes the rain fills up the hole you dug for the 'kleinhuisie' and the pools lie around the shack. Chris Barnard in the *Daily Dispatch* 6.7.81

– From *A Dictionary of South African English*
Jean Branford with William Branford

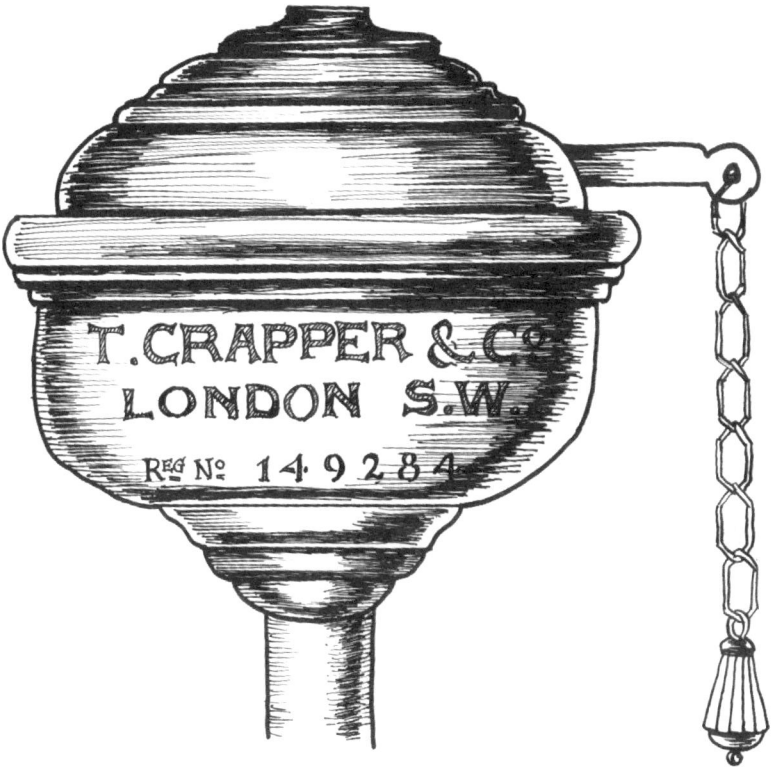

THE FINAL
FLUSH

Here are a few odds and sods to keep you amused in idle moments...

SOME QUOTES

<u>George Moore</u>: A taste for dirty stories may be said to be inherent in the human mind.

<u>Danny la Rue</u>: The essence of any blue material is timing. If you sit on it, it becomes vulgar.

<u>Theophile Gautier</u>: Nothing is really beautiful unless it is useless; everything useful is ugly. The most useful place in a house is the lavatory.

<u>Klaus Kinski</u>: Making movies is better than cleaning toilets.

Mary Wesley, from *Second Fiddle*

He circled back to the town ... to park in a multi-storey car park.

From the top deck of the car park there was a magnificent view of the river, the cathedral-sized church, the market square and distant downland. It was a sign of the age, he thought, as he ran down the steps to the street, that car parks like lavatories often had the best views and, like lavatories, he thought, holding his breath, they stank.

Genuine extracts of letters sent to an English council's maintenance department

Would you please repair our toilet. My son pulled the chain and the box fell on his head.

The lavatory is blocked, this is caused by the boys next door throwing their balls on the roof.

The toilet is blocked and we cannot bath the children until it is cleared.

This is to let you know there is a smell coming from the man next door.

Our lavatory seat is broken in half and is now in three pieces.

This is to let you know that our lavatory seat is broken and we can't get BBC 2.

The toilet seat is cracked. Where do I stand?

VENGEANCE IS MINE...

Voltaire's reply to a gentleman who had written impudently:

I am seated in the smallest room in the house. I have your letter before me. Soon it will be behind me.

Simon Schama, in his elegant tome on the French Revolution, *Citizens*, tells the story of how Louis XVI became so sick of Benjamin Franklin's popularity that, in an effort to make Diana de Polignac cease her constant eulogies of Franklin, he had a Sèvres chamber pot painted with Franklin's image on the inside.

From **Dear Sir, Drop Dead!** *edited by Donald Carroll*

Letter to an upstairs neighbour in Putney, regarding his use of the plumbing:

> I very much regret having to complain, but we are frequently disturbed at a very early hour (5am this morning) and very late at night, by the indiscreet use of your toilets.
>
> The plumbing in this building is very poor and if not used discreetly the tenants below are always aware of the toilets being used, and this coupled with pulling the chain late at night or early morning, is most disturbing and also embarrassing.

Letter to the American Better Business Bureau, a voluntary organisation set up by businessmen which monitors the activities of its members and deals with consumer complaints:

> I want your reaction to a situation that has been developing over the past decade or two which works a hardship upon every person affected with various impediments, such as Arthritis, Broken Limbs, Stiff Knees, Heavy Bodies, and recovery from sickness (weakness). I refer to the prevailing installation of low (and I mean LOW) toilet seats.
>
> They are not only hard to sit down on but HARDER to get up from.
>
> I am speaking from experience. I expect a reply from you.

DOGGY DOINGS

November 24 1978:

The first *public flush-toilets* for dogs were installed at specially selected sites in the streets of Paris. As if this were not luxury enough, the concrete bowls were fitted with tall posts for dogs who preferred more traditional methods.

– From Jeremy Beadle's *Today's the Day! A Chronicle of the Curious*

In 1983, a pair of dog handlers went one step further and came up with a good solution to the problem faced by all owners of small gardens and large dogs. Ruth Golembo of the *Sunday Times* reported on 2 October:

Two inventive men got tired of putting their foot in it – so they've invented a revolutionary new doggy loo. Their plastic bucket solution to the gooey, smelly problem most dog lovers have to contend with has been snapped up by dog owners.

Colin Burger and Dave Quillian, both ex-Rhodesian police dog handlers, have had their enzyme-and-bucket system on the market for only a few weeks, but already the demand has been 'incredible'.

'We both have big dogs of our own... Obviously there are thousands of other dog owners struggling with the same thing. Besides being smelly and unpleasant, dog pooh can be very dangerous. It contains a virus which can cause children to go blind,' Colin said.

The bucket is completely childproof. It seals with a tight-fitting lid and, depending on the size of the dog, it can be used for about two or three weeks before it needs emptying. 'All one has to do is fill the bucket with water and the enzyme ... and scoop in the doggies' daily droppings. The enzyme breaks it down almost completely – leaving only a small layer of silt,' Dave said.

And it doesn't require potty training.

Most dogs look before they leap, but then there are the canine blondes. Margaret de Paravicini passed on this anecdote in her Between the Lines column in *The Star* on 17 November 1990:

> My friend's miniature Maltese, Gabi, has a habit of sitting on the loo seat while her mistress takes a bath. It's cute, but Gabi can't be very bright – the other day, not realising the lid was up, she took a leap and landed in the pan, nearly drowning in the process.

SOME ADVERTISING SLOGANS

First Thing Every Morning Renew Your Health With ENO's – Eno's fruit salts laxative, current in the UK in 1927

Helps You Break The Laxative Habit – Carter's Little Liver Pills, USA, quoted in 1958

Inner cleanliness – the slogan for Andrews Liver Salts, a laxative, current in the UK from the

1950s. 'To complete your inner cleanliness, Andrews cleans the bowels. It sweeps away troublemaking poisons, relieves constipation, and purifies the blood.'

Keep 'Regular' With Ex-Lax – Ex-Lax chocolate laxative, USA, current 1934

– From *The Nigel Rees Book of Slogans & Catchphrases*

AD FADS

It seems that you can't escape advertising anywhere – not even in the toilet. With somewhat muted enthusiasm the *Financial Mail* reported in its Advertising Supplement on 14 July 1989:

CAPTIVE AUDIENCE

Advertising on the back of toilet doors and above urinals has been brought to restaurants, gyms and cinemas by ex advertising man Willem Labuschagne.

He describes his escapade into this rather unusual medium as 'long and hard'. Nor is he taking it lightly. He has 'worked very hard to overcome negative associations with the advertiser's product and the conveniences, using elegant aluminium frames and high quality advertising material.'

Emphasising product benefits to target markets in a, well, captive situation takes on new meaning and Labuschagne has already handled campaigns for the National Association of Child Care Workers and Print Comp Quip. Next in line is an importer of tools...

However, laxatives, loo rolls, pantihose and sanitary protection are also obvious potential products. Labuschagne believes that convenience advertising is a 'trial or action medium for advertisers.'

Agencies appear to have grasped the concept with both hands and are reflecting on their needs.

Ten years later, the result appears to have been more trial than action. Though many of the elegant aluminium frames linger on, they're mostly empty.

Cheetah Haysom's despatches to *The Star* from New York were always entertaining. This one from 9 September 1987 took a look at the stringent controls on American TV advertising:

WHY TOILET BOWLS ON U.S. TV TALK WITH AN ENGLISH ACCENT

American news programmes give graphic details of how you catch AIDS. Documentaries explain in detail the President's bowel surgery. Soap operas show naked couples rolling about under the sheets. You'd think anything goes. And when it comes to ads, there would be no taboo.

But you are wrong. Ads are so rigidly controlled that even when they break up a steamy love scene ... they have to be the apogee of decorum. The networks justify the double standard by saying that advertisements encourage viewers to imitate them, while programming only entertains.

'The most blatant commercials are bland compared to what's on the networks,' says Stephen Novick, an executive of a leading New York advertising agency... 'It's as if when the commercials come on, the viewer is a Victorian,' says the chairman of another New York ad firm...

The rules and regulations are created and enforced by scores of network personnel who spend their days examining commercials as well as programming. Some of the taboos:

Pills: No pill-popping – not even aspirin or cold tablets – is allowed on TV. The networks fear the cumulative effects on viewers.

Passionate kissing: No lingering kisses or open mouths are permitted, not even in mouthwash or toothpaste ads. And most couples in the ads wear wedding rings – to avoid any implications of 'immorality'.

Toilet paper: It is permissible to squeeze it or roll it down the stairs, but networks forbid 'direct or indirect references to product use and function.'

Toilet bowls: Although toilet bowls can now be shown, no water gurgling or flushing is allowed. (At last allowed to show the offensive object on the air, two manufacturers of antiseptic cleaners give their bowls an English accent, to make them seem more respectable).

Eating: No burping, overeating or gluttonous behaviour.

Deodorant: it is forbidden to reveal an underarm, or show the presence of perspiration…

Now we know why there are so many toddling babies in our TV ads. They're experts at rolling toilet paper down the stairs.

Marlene Burger commented in the *Sunday Times* on 5 July 1992:

There's a preponderance of ads for … toilet aids on TV1 just now.

There's busy housewife Gail, whose bowl is so clean she never gives it a second thought; there's something called Big Don and the mildly amusing 'royal flush' sketch, which leans heavily on puns to put the message across. Any day now the flying duck will come hurtling back into our living rooms. Mind you, given the amount of sewage spilt by some of the guests on *Agenda*, and the garbage spewed out each week under the guise of entertainment, perhaps the sanitary ad content is not entirely inappropriate.

FINALLY...

An anecdote from *The Star*'s Stoep Talk on 16 November 1988, when it was written by Olga Horowitz:

As a shining example of what women were doing to help the war effort in Britain in World War II, the wife of Alfred Hitchcock was interviewed by a young reporter. By question and answer they went through her normal day hour by hour, minute by minute. He was elated. What a saga of endurance! ...

'And just one last question: what do you do in your spare time?'

Mrs Hitchcock: 'My dear young man, I go to the lavatory.'

There was a celebrated nineteenth century painter who was a very short man, so he installed a special low lavatory in his home. However, the painter's friends were of normal height, so another standard-height lavatory was installed to cater for their needs.

That's why they called him Two-Loos Lautrec.

Alexander Chase, from *Perspectives*:
Psychiatry's chief contribution to philosophy is the discovery that the toilet is the seat of the soul.

SELECT
BIBLIOGRAPHY

Agatha Christie: an Autobiography (Fontana)

Aussie Etiket – or Doing Things the Aussie Way by John O'Grady (Kaye & Ward)

An Act of Terror by André Brink (Secker & Warburg)

Backhouses of the North by Muriel Newton-White (Highway Book Shop, Cobalt, Ontario)

The Best of P.S. by John Scott (Don Nelson)

A Book at Bathtime by Frank Muir (Coronet)

Bugles & a Tiger by John Masters (Michael Joseph)

Class by Jilly Cooper (Corgi)

Clean and Decent by Lawrence Wright (Routledge)

Cleanliness & Godliness by Reginald Reynolds (George Allen & Unwin)

Cotswold Privies by Mollie Harris (Chatto & Windus - The Hogarth Press)

Dear Sir, Drop Dead! Edited by Donald Carroll (Eyre Methuen)

Dinkum Dunnies by D Baglin & B Mullins (Eclipse)

Flushed with Pride by Wallace Reyburn (Pavilion)

The Frank Muir Book by Frank Muir (Heinemann)

The Geordie Nettie by Frank Graham (Butler & Butler)

Good Neighbours : Suburbia Observed by Richard Gordon (Heinemann)

Handbook for Farmers in South Africa, Department of Agriculture (The Government Printer)

How to Enjoy Your Operation by Vivian Ellis (Frederick Muller)

Jeremy Beadle's Today's the Day! A Chronicle of the Curious (W H Allen)

"Leaky Loos" – And other views... The D.I.Y. book for women by Terry McAllen (McAllen Publications)

Long Walk to Freedom by Nelson Mandela (Little Brown)

The Moon's a Balloon by David Niven (Coronet)

Period Piece by Gwen Raverat (Faber)

A Postillion Struck by Lightning by Dirk Bogarde (Triad Panther)

Privies Galore by Mollie Harris (Alan Sutton)

The Smallest Room by John Pudney (Michael Joseph)

The Specialist by Chic Sale (Putnams) (a 1930 classic)

Temples of Convenience & Chambers of Delight by Lucinda Lambton (Pavilion)

This Day And Age by Mike Nicol (David Philip)

The Toilet Book or 11 ½ minutes a day ... & how not to waste them by Bill Oddie & Laura Beaumont (Methuen)

Thunder, Flush & Thomas Crapper by Adam Hart-Davis (Michael O'Mara)

True Confessions of Adrian Albert Mole by Sue Townsend (Methuen)

Warm and Snug : The History of the Bed by Lawrence Wright (Routledge)

Unreliable Memoirs by Clive James (Picador)

Where's All the White Air Gone? by John Scott (Don Nelson)

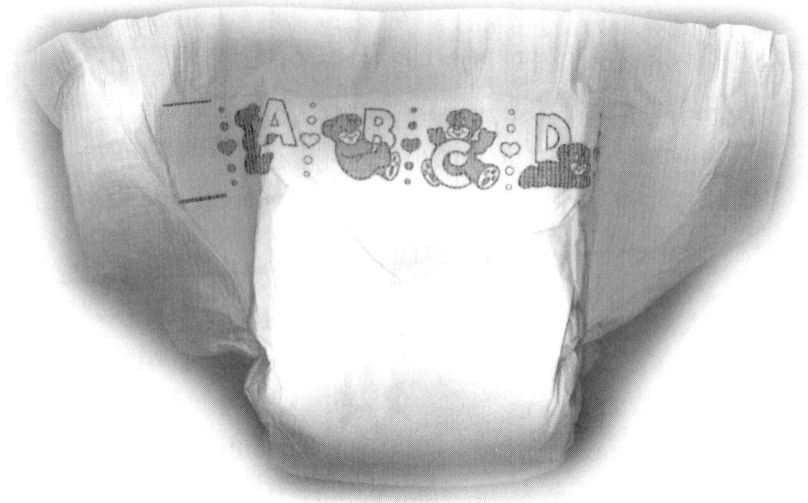

GENTLE READERS

We would welcome contributions to a possible second edition, especially literary extracts, photographs, cartoons, droll anecdotes and stories with a South African slant.
Send them to

Pees and Queues
Spearhead Press
P O Box 75360
Gardenview
2047

with a line giving us permission to use them.